Marriages
of
Sussex County
Virginia

- 1754-1810 -

Compiled By:
Catherine Lindsay Knorr

Southern Historical Press, Inc.
Greenville, South Carolina

SOUTHERN HISTORICAL PRESS, INC.
PO BOX 1267
Greenville, SC   29601

ISBN #0-89308-257-0

Printed in the United States of America

To

Those able and generous

genealogists from whom

I have learned so much and

to whom I owe so much more

(alphabetically arranged, gentlemen!)

Arthur Adams

John I. Coddington

Meredith B. Colket, Jr.

John Goodwin Herndon

Donald Lines Jacobus

George H. S. King

Milton Rubincam

JAMES CITY 1634 (ORIGINAL SHIRE)
|
SURRY 1652
|
SUSSEX 1755-54

James River

Prince
George

Dinwiddie

Surry

SUSSEX
⊙

Isle
of
Wight

Brunswick

Southampton

Greensville

Publisher's Preface

Mrs. Knorr died in 1975, and after her death these books of marriage records were kept in print and sold by her late husband. Upon his death, they became the property of her grandson, Hal Wyche Greer, III, of Marietta, Georgia, who continued to sell them on a limited basis.

In mid-1981 I sought to find Mr. Greer to discuss with him the possibility of obtaining the exclusive publishing and sales rights to these 14 titles. In due time, Mr. Greer and I were able to negotiate a contract for my exclusive sales and publication rights to these books. It was agreed that Mr. Greer would have a final voice on the changing of the format of any of these titles when they needed to be reprinted. I suggested to Mr. Greer that when these various books sold out and a reprinting had to be done, that for the sake of cost, I would publish them in a 6" x 9" page size, but that the format and style would remain the same, and this was agreed upon.

The reader is cautioned to note that these new 6 x 9 pages are typed verbatum from Mrs. Knorr's original copy, and page by page, so that new indexing was not required. It was also decided that when a book went out of print, it would be retyped on an electric typewriter with a carbon ribbon for better legibility. As publisher, I felt it was important to call to the attention of the reader these changes and the reason for eventually bringing out all of these titles in a 6 x 9 book.

The Rev. S. Emmett Lucas, Jr.
Publisher

PREFACE

Honestly, there is nothing so peaceful as a Virginia Court House. One cannot associate with their present day tranquility any scenes of strife, bitter legal battles or heated debates. Sussex is a shining example of the calm that prevails under the shade of giant old oaks.

The first to welcome one is usually a nobly beautiful bird dog who advances with waving plume and trusting friendliness in his limpid eyes. Too dignified to be effusive he does his duty as a gentleman and a host, then retires to his shady spot again.

Next a deputy clerk who greets one then the clerk himself. The pattern is always the same, and it is one not to be tampered with. It is perfect just as it is.

The clerk, Mr. William B. Cocke, Jr., makes it very plain that one is welcome to work in his Sussex County records, so copying begins.

Surry County first saw English colonists 5 May 1607. Capt. George Percy reports "Fine paths in the woods, most pleasant springs and the goodliest corn fields I have seen in any country." Surry was part of the original shire, James City County, until 1652 when it was set up as a new county. Surry, a long narrow county running northeast and southwest was bisected by the Blackwater River which later became the dividing line between Surry and Sussex. North of that body of water was well settled by 1700, but the territory south of Blackwater was not legally opened for settlement until 1710. (Hening's Statutes Vol. IV, p. 546).

The Council had ordered on 23 August 1702 that the land south of Blackwater be laid open after November 20th, and that all her Majestie's subjects should have liberty to take up and patent land there.

In 1753 a petition was handed to the general assembly from the inhabitants of Surry County living south of the Blackwater for the erection of a new county. On 1 February 1754 an act for the creation of Sussex County became effective. (Hening's Statutes Vol. VI p. 384). The severance was natural and logical; vast distances had delayed legal accomplishments as well as religious affairs in Surry.

In 1752 Virginia was divided into four military districts each with its own officer. Sussex, falling into the Southern District, was commanded by Col. George Washington. On his expedition to acquaint the French with the Colony's plans to fortify the western frontier of Virginia the 21 year old Washington was joined by such Sussex men as Capt. Henry Harrison and Capt. James Wyche.

Albemarle Parish, formed from Southwark and Lawne's Creek Parishes on 1 November 1738 had as vestrymen in 1754, when Sussex was formed, Robert Jones, Jr., Thomas Avent, James Chappell, Moses Johnson, Ephraim Parham, Augustine Claiborne, James Gee, Howell Briggs and John Mason, Jr.

The first Burgesses who represented Sussex County in the General Assembly of 14 February 1754 were Gray Briggs and John Edmunds. John Ruffin replaced John Edmunds who accepted a surveyor's place, 22 August 1754. (Stanard's Colonial Virginia Register p. 131 and 133).

The first Gentleman Justices were: John Avent, James Jones, William Lightfoot, James Mason, John Mason, Nicholas Massenburg, Edward Pettway, Thomas Vines, James Wyche, John Wyche, Howell Briggs, and James Gee.

The first Clerk was Augustine Claiborne and the first Sheriff was James Chappell.

It is a pleasure to report that Sussex was a center for horse racing in Colonial days. Blooded racing stock was being imported and such champions as Jolly Roger, Silver Heels, Merry Tom, Sterling, Aristotle and Fearnaught were Sussex owned and raced in Sussex.

To the Revolutionary Army Sussex gave 1 general, 12 colonels, 3 majors, 17 captains, 8 lieutenants, 2 surgeons, and numerous lesser officers as well as privates.

It is impossible to over estimate the importance of Sussex in the history and development of Virginia and of America.

                              Catherine Lindsay Knorr

Mrs. H.A. Knorr
1401 Linden Street
Pine Bluff, Arkansas

5 April 1792. James ABERNATHY and Elizabeth Cain. Sur. John Powell. p. 67.

2 May 1793. James ABERNATHY and Beckey Wilborn. Married 16 May by Rev. William Brown. Sur. Benjamin Wilborn. p. 71.

2 October 1806. Jesse ABERNATHY and Rebecca Jackson, dau. Francis Jackson. Sur. Burwell Jackson. Wit: Benjamin Harris, Harris Wilborne and Frederick Jackson. p. 121.

30 April 1805. Amos ADAMS and Sally Evans. Married 4 May by Rev. James Rogers. Sur. Jesse Wrenn. p. 117.

3 December 1789. Benjamin ADAMS and Mima (Jemima?) Williamson, dau. Mary Williamson. Sur. Amos Adams. p. 57.

29 January 1802. Benjamin ADAMS and Elizabeth Hails, dau. Susanna Hails. Sur. Joel Hails. Married by Rev. Stith Parham. p. 105.

30 September 1800. Charles ADAMS and Sarah Waller. Sur. James McLemore. p. 98.

23 August 1806. Claiborne ADAMS and Polly Zills, dau. Rebecca Zills. Married 26 August by Rev. Robert Murrell, Sr. Sur. Benjamin Hogwood. Wit: Charles Hogwood. Ministers' returns say Polly Sils. p. 121.

6 April 1809. Henry ADAMS and Nancy Robertson, orphan. Married 12 April by Rev. Robert Murrell, Sr., of Shouthampton Co. Sur. Henry R. Gilliam. p. 132.

28 March 1778. Isaac ADAMS, Jr., and Susanna Wingfield, dau. William Wingfield. Isaac son of Isaac Adams, Sr. Isaac Jr. of Brunswick County. Sur. Augustine Claiborne. Wit: Richard Hill and Thomas Hill. p. 24.

3 July 1790. Isaac ADAMS and Nancy Williamson. Married 4 July by Rev. John Meglamore. Sur. Benjamin Bullock. p. 60.

5 July 1792. Isaac ADAMS and Olive Mabry. Sur. Amos Adams. Married by Rev. William Brown. p. 67.

26 February 1760. James ADAMS and Ann Harper, widow of Wiatt Harper. Sur. John Hudson. p. 5.

19 July 1791. John ADAMS and Mary Pate, dau. Thomas Pate who is surety. p. 63.

13 September 1796. John ADAMS and Phoebe Mabry. Married 15 September by Rev. Stith Parham. Sur. Abel Mabry. p. 83.

11 January 1802. Jordan ADAMS and Ann Pettway. Sur. Weathers
Adams, p. 105.

13 October 1803. Jordan ADAMS and Fanny Waller. Sur. Joel Hails.
p. 112.

18 October 1808. Jordan ADAMS and Ann Zills. Sur. James Bendall.
Married 20 October by Rev. James Rogers who says Ann Sills.
p. 129.

28 March 1810. Pennington W. ADAMS and Polly Hood, dau. Lucretia
Hood. Sur. William H. Coleman. p. 135.

2 November 1792. Weathers ADAMS and Judy Bendall, ward of William
Massenburg. Sur. Jesse Zills. Married 15 November by Rev. Henry
Moss who says Judah. p. 68.

27 September 1786. William ADAMS and Nancy Turner. Sur. Vines
Turner. p. 43.

30 April 1792. Winfield ADAMS and Martha Cain. Sur. Claiborne
Cain. Married by Rev. George Parham. p. 67.

1 June 1782. Howel ADKINS and Susanna Lucas, ward of John
Berryman. Sur. Richard Cook. Wit: Balaam Berryman and Josiah
Berryman. p. 30.

23 February 1796. Howell ADKINS and Elizabeth Heath. Married
25 February by Rev. Henry Moss. Sur. John Moss. p. 81.

3 January 1793. William ADKINS and Susanna Lanier. Married
7 January by Rev. Henry Moss. Sur. John Graves. p. 70.

13 July 1793. Willis ADKINS and Rebecca Graves. Sur. David
Graves. Wit: Benjamin B. Rosser. p. 71.

17 November 1810. Thomas ALDRIDGE and Peggy Richardson, consent
of Mary Richardson. Sur. John Whitehorn. p. 137.

28 December 1801. Benjamin ALLEN and Polly Wilborne. Married
7 January 1802 by Rev. James Rogers. Sur. John Love. p. 104.

20 March 1775. Edward ANDERSON and Susanna Oliver, dau. William
Oliver who is surety. p. 21.

13 February 1800. James ANDERSON and Martha Chappell, dau.
Thomas Chappel. Married 20 February by Rev. Stith Parham.
Sur. Thomas Malone. Wit: Tinsley Heath and Phoebe Tucker.
p. 96.

28 October 1784. McDuell ANDERSON and Jane Sykes. Sur. William
Sykes. p. 35.

11 July 1803. Nelson ANDERSON and Sarah Johnson. Returned 3
May 1804 by Rev. Joseph Hill. Sur. Henry Wilkerson. p. 112.

5 June 1810. Thomas ANDERSON and Frances Shands, dau. William
Shands, Sr. Thomas Anderson of Chesterfield County. Sur.
Calvin Hine. p. 136.

12 February 1790. Blackburn ANDREWS and Elizabeth Barker. Sur.
Henry Barker. p. 59.

17 February 1785. Henry ANDREWS and Betsy Holt, dau. Nathaniel
Holt. Sur. Person Williamson. Wit: Levi Gilliam. p. 36.

25 April 1807. Isaac ANDREWS and Patsy Loftin. Married 30 April
by Rev. James Rogers. Sur. Jonathan Harrup. p. 125.

4 December 1806. John ANDREWS and Patsy Cross, dau. John Cross.
Married 18 December by Rev. Drury Lane. Sur. John Potts. p. 122.

20 January 1801. Joseph ANDREWS and Susanna Ellis, dau. John
Ellis. Joseph Andrews nephew of Drewry Lane. Married 29
January by Rev. Drewry Lane. Sur. John Owen. p. 100.

20 January 1806. Richard ANDREWS and Polley Bailey. Married
23 January by Rev. Drury Lane. Sur. Joseph Andrews. p. 119.

7 April 1796. Stephen ANDREWS and Elizabeth Ellis, consent of
Benjamin Ellis. Married 14 April by Rev. Drewry Lane. Sur.
Benjamin Tomlinson. Wit: Benjamin W. Johnson and J.C. Bailey.
p. 81.

10 December 1792. William ANDREWS and Sally Pleasants. Sur.
William Pleasants. p. 69.

21 June 1796. Amos ATKINS and Phebe Ezell. Married 24 June by
Rev. Stith Parham. Sur. Frederick Mabry. p. 82.

15 July 1791. John ATKINS and Molley Hay. Sur. Richard Hay.
p. 63.

15 December 1800. Jesse ATKINSON and Nancy Layne (Lane).
Married 18 December by Rev. Drewry Lane who says Nancy Lane.
Sur. John Lain. Wit: Sally Lain. p. 99.

23 January 1807. Johnson ATKINSON and Clotilda White. Married
29 January by Rev. Drewry Lane. Sur. James Coker. p. 123.

5 October 1781. William ATKINSON and Wlizabeth Brantley. Sur.
Mark Carrell. p. 29.

12 November 1787. Lemuel ATKISON (Adkins) and Patty Carrell,
dau. Mrs. Priscilla Britt. Sur. John Hart. Wit: John Britt.
p. 48.

19 January 1786. Benjamin AVENT and Lucy Grizzard. Sur. William
Grizzard. p. 41.

31 May 1766. John AVERY and Ann Hill, widow. Sur. Banester
Shackleford. p. 10.

30 January 1798. Burwell BACON and Anney Kelley. Sur. Charles Mitchell. p. 88.

21 January 1790. Joseph Mosby BACON and Mary Vines, ward of Green Hill. Sur. John Vines. Married by Rev. George Parham. p. 59.

22 September 1794. Benjamin BAILEY and Rebecca Carter. Benjamin son of Thomas Bailey. Sur. Henry Hawthorne. p. 74.

15 January 1789. Brittain BAILEY and Lucy Andrews, dau. Henry Andrews. Married 5 February by Rev. John Meglamore. Sur. Balaam Freeman. Wit: John Blunt. p. 54.

29 October 1803. Charles BAILEY and Rebecca Lain, consent of Jesse Lain. Married 17 November by Rev. Drewry Lane who says Lane. Sur. John Lane. Wit: James Bailey. p. 112.

2 March 1802. Edmund BAILEY and Rebecca Clanton, dau. Mrs. Sally Whitehorn. Sur. Wyatt Bailey. Married by Rev. Stith Parham. p. 106.

30 November 1805. Harmon BAILEY and Susan Sledge. Sur. Miles Sledge. p. 118.

23 December 1802. James BAILEY and Sally Lane, dau. Drewry Lane. Married by Rev. Samuel Risher. Sur. Lemuel Hargrave. Wit: Robert Lane and Patsy Lane. p. 109.

1 December 1803. James C. BAILEY and Eliza S. Wood. Married by Rev. James Rogers. p. 112.

26 January 1792. John BAILEY and Rebecca Bailey, consent of James Wright who is surety. Wit: Benjamin Wyche. p. 66.

2 November 1809. John BAILEY and Rhoda Holloway. Married 30 November by Rev. Drewry Lane. Sur. William Pleasants. p. 134.

15 April 1784. Joseph BAILEY and Mary Blow. Joseph Bailey of Surry County. Sur. Michael Blow. p. 35.

7 September 1799. Joseph G. BAILEY and Sally Blow. Sur. Lemuel Bailey. p. 94.

2 February 1809. Laban BAILEY and Lucy G. Hewitt. Married 8 February by Rev. James Rogers. Sur. William H. Niblett. p. 131.

3 February 1784. Peter BAILEY and Mary Hobbs. Peter Bailey of Southampton County. Married February 12 by Rev. John Meglamore. Sur. James Bailey. p. 34.

2 January 1794. Philip BAILEY and Betsy Meglamore. Married by Rev. William Brown. Ministers' Returns p. 269.

17 October 1796. Philip BAILEY and Susahhan Cotton. Sur. Richard Bailey. p. 84.

12 January 1786. Richard BAILEY and Drucilla Cotten. Married by Rev. John Meglamore. Ministers' Returns p. 258.

16 January 1789. Robert BAILEY and Elizabeth Chappell. Married 19 January by Rev. John Meglamore. Sur. John Chappell. p. 54.

20 December 1800. Samuel BAILEY and Sally Lane, consent of Jesse Lane. Married 25 December by Rev. Drewry Lane. Sur. Samuel Lane. Wit: Lucy Lane. p. 99.

12 October 1780. Thomas BAILEY and Mary Hancock, widow. Sur. Thomas Phillips. Wit: Mary Booth. p. 26.

21 July 1809. Thomas BAILEY and Aggy Morriss. Sur. William A. Stacy. Wit: Thomas Faison. p. 133.

26 October 1785. Wyatt BAILEY and Phebey Woodland. Married by Rev. John Meglamore. Ministers' Returns p. 258.

18 March 1807. Elijah BAIN and Rhoda Brock, consent of James Brock. Sur. Lemuel Bain. p. 124.

19 December 1781. John BAIN and Sylvia Wooten, dau. Edward Wooten. Sur. Nicholas Presson. Wit: Ann Wooten. p. 29.

13 October 1808. Lemuel BAIN and Lucy Murrell. Married 20 October by Rev. Drewry Lane. Sur. Henry W. Carrell. p. 129.

11 December 1802. Samuel BAINE and Nancy Booth. Married 23 December by Rev. Drewry Lane. Sur. Zaccheus Baine. p. 109.

12 June 1806. Benjamin BAINES and Sally Hicks. Sur. Reuben Freeman. p. 121.

28 January 1804. Zaccheus BAINES and Jincey Murphey. Sur. Jenkins Murphey. Wit: Peter Booth. p. 113.

18 March 1785. Benjamin BAIRD and Mary Grizzard, dau. Ambrose Grizzard, deceased. Sur. Stephen Baird. Wit: John Cocke. p. 37.

9 April 1802. George BAIRD and Mariah Ivey. Married 10 April by Rev. Augustine Heath. Sur. Daniel Grant. p. 106.

18 December 1792. Hamlin BAIRD and Mary Edwards. Sur. William Harrison. p. 69.

6 December 1810. John BAIRD and Susan Redding. Sur. John Ambrose. Wit: Levina Ambrose. p. 137.

16 September 1779. William BAIRD and Rebecca Edwards, widow. Sur. Jesse Ivey. p. 25.

26 November 1761. Burwell BANKS and Mary Mason. Sur. Thomas Tomlinson. p. 6.

20 May 1785. James BANKS and Elizabeth Parham, widow of Thomas Parham. Sur. Richard Mason. p. 37.

24 November 1801. Benjamin BARHAM and Sally Rochell, dau. Hinchia Rochell. Sur. Edward Pennington. p. 103.

2 July 1798. Howell BARHAM and Anna Long. Sur. David Long. p. 90.

24 July 1785. Robert BARHAM and Susanna Winney. Married by Rev. John Meglamore. Ministers' Returns p. 258.

17 January 1780. Hartwell BARHAM and Seesela (Cecelia?) Freeman. Sur. George Bell. Wit: Benjamin Johnson. p. 25.

11 February 1791. Burwell BARKER and Nancy Barker. Sur. William Barker. Married by Rev. John Meglamore. p. 63.

18 August 1796. David BARKER and Hannah Sammons, dau. Thomas Sammons. Sur. Curtis Lynne. p. 83.

3 November 1785. Gray BARKER and Elizabeth Gilbert, dau. James Gilbert who is surety. Married 11 December by Rev. John Meglamore. p. 40.

29 April 1783. James BARKER and Joanne Andrews, consent of Stephen and Lydia Andrews. Sur. Jesse Barker. Wit: Susanna Andrews. p. 32.

29 January 1765. Jehu BARKER and Lucy Place. Sur. Thomas Wallace. Wit: David Jones. p. 9.

2 November 1795. Richard BARKER and Nancy Andrews, consent of Mary Andrews. Married 22 December by Rev. Drewry Lane. Sur. Stephen Andrews. p. 79.

8 January 1803. Thomas BARKER and Lucy Ellis, dau. John Ellis. Married 13 January by Rev. Drewry Lane. Sur. Archibald W. Bowles. p. 109.

5 January 1809. Henry M. BASS and Polly Owen. Married 11 January by Rev. James Rogers. Sur. William Thornton. p. 131.

7 December 1809. Howell BASS and Silviah Manry, dau. Peter Manry. Married 3 January 1810 by Rev. Robert Murrell, Sr. of Southampton Co. Sur. David Newsom. p. 134.

18 August 1785. Frederick BATTS and Tabitha Mitchell. Sur. David Mason. Married 13 September by Rev. Jesse Lee. p. 38.

4 June 1795. Frederick BATTS and Margaret Bonner, dau. John
Bonner, Sr. Sur. Henry Bass. Wit: John Bonner, Jr. p. 77.

28 January 1788. Robert BAUGH and Martha (Patsy) Cleveland.
Robert Baugh under age, ward of Peter Williamson. Sur. William
Harrison. p. 50.

27 July 1792. John BEDINGFIELD and Polly Cook. Sur. Richard
Cook. p. 67.

1 February 1766. Hugh BELSCHER and Martha Avery, dau. Richard
Avery. Sur. Augustine Claiborne. Wit: Susanna Claiborne. p. 10.

8 October 1792. Benjamin BELL and Elizabeth Powell, dau. John
Powell. Married 18 October by Rev. William Brown. Sur. Edward
Powell. Wit: Thomas Fletcher. p. 68.

3 September 1801. James BELL and Martha Graves. Sur. David Graves.
p. 102.

3 March 1792. John BELL and Elizabeth Loftin, dau. William
Loftin. Married 8 March by Rev. William Brown. Sur. Jonathan
Harrup. p. 66.

20 April 1769. Silvanus BELL and Mary Johnson, dau. Lewis Johnson.
Sur. James Bell. Wit: A. Freeman and John Heron. p. 13.

8 March 1796. Isaac BENDALL and Sally Rose, dau. Richard Rose.
Sur. Joseph N. Meredith. p. 81.

14 February 1784. John BERRIMAN, Jr. and Mary Lamb, dau. John
Lamb. Sur. Abraham Jones. Wit: Littleberry Jones. p. 34.

30 December 1789. Andrew BETTS and Sally White, dau. James White.
Sur. Warren White. p. 58.

28 February 1763. William BIGGINS and Molly Biggins, dau. Sara
Biggins, widow. Sur. Nathaniel Mitchell. Sur. Charles Harrison
and Mary Harrison. p. 7.

21 December 1809. Benjamin BIRDSONG and Polly C. Cotton. Married
26 December by Rev. Drewry Lane. Sur. John Jarrad. p. 135.

17 November 1803. George BIRDSONG and Nancy Mason, dau. Thomas
Mason. Married 23 November by Rev. James Rogers. Sur. William
Birdsong. p. 112.

22 June 1801. John BIRDSONG and Nancy Jarrad. Married 25 June
by Rev. Drewry Lane. Sur. Joseph Jarrad. Double wedding: see
Thomas Birdsong. p. 101.

13 December 1806. John BIRDSONG and Lucy Mason, dau. Thomas Mason.
Married 18 December by Rev. James Rogers. Sur. Samuel Birdsong.
p. 122.

5 January 1799. Joseph BIRDSONG and Cherry Hargrave. Married 13 January by Rev. Drewry Lane. Sur. Isaac Hill. p. 92.

24 May 1808. Samuel BIRDSONG and Jiney H. Land. Married 26 May by Rev. Drewry Lane who says Jincy H. Land. Sur. Henry Chappell. p. 128.

22 June 1801. Thomas BIRDSONG and Rebecca Jarrad. Married 25 June by Rev. Drewry Lane. Sur. Joseph Jarrad. Double wedding; see John Birdsong. p. 101.

3 May 1781. William BIRDSONG and Susanna Jones, dau. Nathaniel Jones. Sur. Augustine Claiborne. Wit: Miles Birdsong, Howell Jones and William Jones. p. 28.

10 June 1799. William BIRDSONG and Mary Nicholson (widow). Married 13 June by Rev. Drewry Lane. Sur. Joseph Birdson. p. 93.

20 April 1790. Augustine BISHOP and Nancy Rawlings. Sur. Stephen Bishop. p. 60.

24 November 1792. Benjamin BISHOP and Elizabeth Bracey. Married 28 November by Rev. Henry Moss. Sur. William Moss. p. 69.

12 February 1799. John BISHOP and Martha Gilliam. Sur. Gray Felts. p. 93.

21 March 1798. Hardaman BISHOP and Lucy Mangam, dau. Samuel Mangam. Sur. William Mangam. Married by Rev. Stith Parham. p. 89.

15 June 1785. Thomas BISHOP and Mary Seymour Dagleish Roberts, dau. William Roberts. Sur. Henry Barker. Wit: Richard Bagwell and Nancy Bagwell. p. 38.

26 December 1803. Thomas BISHOP and Lucy Lilly. Married 29 December by Rev. James Rogers. Sur. Philip Bailey. p. 113.

22 June 1803. John BLIZZARD and Polly Byrd. Married 23 June by Rev. Drewry Lane. Sur. Drewry Taylor. Wit: G. Himes. p. 111.

18 April 1809. Alexander BLOW and Elizabeth Jarrad. Married 20 April by Rev. Drewry Lane. Sur. Henry Little. p. 132.

11 February 1771. Henry BLOW and Rebecca Birdsong, dau. John Birdsong. Sur. William Brittle. Wit: Miles Birdsong and Jone Rives. p. 14.

17 June 1763. John BLOW and Mary Briggs, dau. George Briggs. John Blow age 21 on 7 July 1762, ward of John Thomas of Southampton County. Sur. Frederick Parker. Wit: Peter Batts and George Briggs. p. 8.

10 May 1798. Micajah BLOW and Sally Parker, dau. Richard Parker. Sur. Thomas A. Blow. p. 90.

22 September 1801. Micajah BLOW and Rebecca Birdsong. Married 1 October by Rev. Drewry Lane. Sur. Edmund Parker. p. 102.

29 November 1766. Benjamin BLUNT and Frances Briggs, dau. George Briggs. Sur. Joseph Rosser. Wit: John Powell, John Edmunds and Howell Briggs. Benjamin Blunt of Southampton County, son of Richard Blunt, deceased, and ward of Howell Edmunds. p. 10.

28 February 1805. Richard BLUNT and Mary E. Massenburg, dau. William Massenburg. Sur. Benjamin B. Rosser. p. 117.

22 November 1796. Samuel BLUNT and Elizabeth Woolfold. Sur. Charles Nicholson. p. 84.

11 November 1783. Thomas BLUNT and Elizabeth Peete, dau. Dr. Thomas Peete. Sur. Nathan Jones. Wit: Benjamin Peete and Martha Riddick. p. 33.

31 December 1789. Thomas BLUNT and Judith Rives, dau. George Rives. Sur. George Rives, Jr. p. 58.

22 April 1807. Thomas BLUNT, Jr. and Anges Archer Downman. Sur. Robert Downman. p. 125.

17 December 1756. William BLUNT and Ann Nicholson, dau. Robert Nicholson who is surety. p. 2.

19 November 1764. William BLUNT and Martha Peete, dau. Dr. Samuel Peete. Sur. Augustine Claiborne. p. 9.

20 March 1788. John BOBBITT and Mary Gilliam. Married 3 April by Rev. John Meglamore. Sur. Isham Gilliam. p. 50.

19 September 1792. John BOBBITT and Frances Mitchell. Sur. Edward Pennington. Married by Rev. John Cameron of Bristol Parish. Returned 11 October 1792. p. 68.

29 October 1777. James BOISSEAU and Mary Jones, consent of David Jones. Sur. John Jones. Wit: Susannah Jones. p. 23.

8 October 1776. Stith BOLLING and Charlotte Edmunds, dau. John Edmunds, deceased and ward of William Blunt. Sur. Thomas Edmunds. Wit: Lucretia Jones and Robert Jones, Jr. p. 21.

14 April 1789. Robert BONDS and Sarah Adams. Married 19 April by Rev. John Meglamore. Sur. Benjamin Phipps. p. 55.

13 August 1787. Chappell BONNER and Priscilla Smith, dau. Isham Smith. Sur. Williamson Smith. p. 47.

1 March 1804. Harry BONNER and Polly Norton. Married 28 March by Rev. Augustine Heath. Sur. Daniel Nives. p. 114.

20 April 1773. James BONNER and Mary Jones, dau. James Jones. Sur. Jeremiah Bonner. p. 17.

4 August 1772. Jeremiah BONNER and Sally Hall, dau. James Hall who is surety. Married by the Rev. John Meglamore. Returned 10 October. p. 15.

9 February 1756. John BONNER and Mary Briggs, widow. Sur. William Bonner. p. 1.

3 February 1791. John BONNER, Jr. and Sarah Smith, dau. Isham Smith. Sur. John Peebles. Married by Rev. John Mason. p. 62.

24 January 1792. Jones BONNER and Elizabeth Malone, consent of Michael Malone. Married 26 January by the Rev. Jesse Lee. Sur. Abraham Lee. p. 66.

7 April 1783. Richard BONNER and Frances Mitchell, dau. Mrs. Prissila Northington. Richard Bonner of Prince George County. Sur. Joshua Young. Wit: Joel Rives. p. 32.

23 December 1806. George BOOTH and Nancy Magee, dau. Willey Maggee. Married 26 December by the Rev. James Rogers. Sur. John Spain. p. 123.

7 June 1810. George BOOTH and Phebe Gilliam. Sur. Howell Cooper. p. 136.

2 April 1795. Gilliam BOOTH and Mary Mason. Sur. John Massenburg. p. 77.

20 June 1782. Michael BOOTH and Celia Barker. Sur. James Bailey. p. 30.

22 October 1792. Robert BOOTH and Phebe Johnson, ward of Lawrence Smith. Sur. James Johnson. p. 68.

15 October 1800. Thomas BOOTH and Polly Cocke. Sur. John Hunt. p. 98.

21 July 1791. John BOTTOM and Mary Hunnicutt. Sur. Glaister Hunnicutt. p. 63.

4 October 1792. Samuel BOTTOM and Lucy Davis. Married 18 October by the Rev. William Brown. Sur. Matthew Davis. p. 68.

5 December 1799. Archibald W. BOWLES and Rowany Barker, dau. Elizabeth Barker. Married 12 December by the Rev. Robert Murrell, Sr. of Southampton Co. Sur. Frederick Cooper. Double wedding; see Frederick Cooper. p. 95.

14 April 1807. Fitzhugh BOWLES and Lucy Barker. Married 16 April by Rev. Drewry Lane. Sur. Drury Kitchen. Wit: Rowana Bowles. p. 124.

18 December 1793. William BRADLEY and Sarah Gilliam. Sur. Carter Gilliam. p. 73.

16 April 1803. Valentine BRANCH and Willey White. Married 23 April by Rev. Drewry Lane. Sur. Samuel White. p. 110.

20 November 1806. William BRANTON and Susanna Thrift. Married by Rev. James Gibbons. Ministers' Returns p. 284.

19 April 1779. William BRENT and Mary Parham, widow. Sur. Gray Burrough. Wit: John Cocke. P. 24.

10 February 1790. Charles BRIGGS, Jr. and Jane Parker, dau. Richard Parker. Sur. Joseph Rosser. p. 59.

17 September 1805. Henry BRIGGS and Sarah Nicholson. Married 26 September by Rev. Drewry Lane. Sur. Benjamin B. Rosser. p. 118.

21 November 1808. Jacob BRIGGS and Jane Wilson. Sur. Frederick Jones. p. 130.

17 August 1791. James BRIGGS and Rhoda Hicks. Sur. Joseph Rosser. p. 63.

18 December 1799. John BRIGGS and Elizabeth Mason Chappell, dau. Elizabeth Chappell. Married 19 December by Rev. Drewry Lane. Sur. Thomas Chappell. p. 95.

19 June 1798. Samuel BRIGGS and Betsy Blow. Sur. Thomas E. Scott. p. 90.

24 May 1762. William BRIGGS and Mary Cooke, dau. Reubin Cooke. Sur. Hinchia Gilliam. p. 7.

1 June 1802. William BRIGGS and Polly Nicholson, dau. Lucy Nicholson. Married 3 June by Rev. Drewry Lane. Sur. Joseph Rosser. p. 107.

Between March 1791 and March 1792. Robert BRISTO and Nancy Green. Married by Rev. William Brown. Ministers' Returns p. 266.

18 April 1810. Willie BRITT and Sally Freeman. Sur. William Clanton. p. 136.

4 May 1798. Britain BRITTLE and Polly Faison. Married 8 May by Rev. Drewry Lane. Sur. Peter Booth. p. 90.

5 January 1789. James BRITTLE and Mary Gay. Sur. Simon Gay. p. 54.

25 August 1796. Henry BROWN and Patty Eggleston. Married by Rev. Stith Parham. Sur. William Brown. Wit: Stith Parham. p. 83.

17 March 1758. Lewis BROWN and Martha Richardson, dau. William
Richardson, deceased. Sur. William Richardson. p. 3.

5 November 1801. John BROWN and Rebecca Rose. Sur. John Holt.
p. 103.

22 June 1802. Thomas BROWN and Patsy Birdsong. Married 24 June
by Rev. Drewry Lane. Sur. James Scammell. p. 107.

5 July 1809. William BROWN and Elizabeth E. Smith. Married by
Rev. James Rogers. Sur. Miles Clary. p. 133.

19 June 1781. John BRYAR and Sarah Baines, widow. Sur. Robert
Lamb. p. 28.

29 December 1784. Tavinor Bird BUFORD and Elizabeth McLin Parham,
dau. Matthew Parham. Sur. James Parham. Wit: William Hering. p. 36.

3 November 1796. Benjamin BULLOCK and Polly Jordan. Sur. John
Pate. p. 84.

22 June 1763. Drury BURGE and Elizabeth Dunn, dau. William Dunn
who is surety. Wit: Joseph Kirkland and John Wynne. Drury Burge
of Dinwiddie Co., son of John Burge. p. 8.

19 March 1804. Joel BURGE and Elizabeth Bass. Married 9 April by
Rev. James Rogers. Sur. Thomas Eldridge. p. 114.

17 December 1785. William BURGE and Rebecca Hall, dau. James
Hall. Sur. Jesse Wrenn. Wit: William Bobbett and John Tyus. Married
22 December by Rev. John Cameron of Bristol Parish. Double wedding: see Jesse Wrenn. p. 41.

1 June 1795. Miles BURGES and Nancy Velvin. Sur. William Velvin.
Married 25 June by Rev. Drewry Lane who says Vilvan. p. 77.

Between 25 September 1771 and 10 October 1772. Henry John BURGESS
and Judith Driver. Married by Rev. John Meglamore. Ministers'
returns p. 257.

12 October 1783. Thomas BURK and Mary Owen. Married by Rev.
John Meglamore. Ministers' Returns p. 322.

23 June 1795. Allen Jones BURROW and Nancy Wilkinson, dau. Nathan
Wilkerson. Sur. Thomas Wilkerson. p. 77.

5 November 1789. Balaam BURROW and Mary Wade Woodard. Sur. Mason
Howell. p. 57.

22 July 1786. Harwood BURT and Rebecca Cross. Sur. Edward Burt.
Wit: Benjamin Wyche. p. 43.

12

7 January 1802. Herod BURT and Martha Coker. Married by Rev.
Drewry Lane. Sur. Drewry Lane. Wit: James Davis, Isaac Felts and
John Davis. p. 105.

7 January 1802. John BUSH and Sally Munds. Sur. Edmund Underwood.
p. 105.

30 November 1809. John BUTLER and Martha Lee. Sur. Thomas Malone,
Jr. p. 134.

20 June 1765. Thomas BUTLER and Mary Norris, infant (under age).
Sur. David Tucker. p. 9.

25 November 1786. William BUTLER and Elizabeth Taylor, widow of
James Taylor. Married 2 December by Rev. Jesse Lee. Sur. Nicholas
Ogburn. p. 44.

19 October 1797. Daniel BUTTS and Mary Blunt Parker, dau. Richard
Parker. Sur. Robert Goodwyn. p. 86.

7 December 1808. James BUTTS and Martha J. Gilliam, dau. Carter
Gilliam. Married 8 December by Rev. James Rogers. Sur. Richard
C. Gilliam. p. 130.

6 March 1784. Allen CAIN and Sarah Wilburne. Sur. Peter Cain.
p. 34.

4 November 1802. Isham CAIN and Rebecca Hawthorn, dau. Joshua
Hawthorn. Sur. Curtis Winfield. Wit: Thomas Shands and William
Parham. Married by Rev. Joseph Hill. p. 108.

29 August 1793. Marston CAIN and Janey Hudson. Married 5 September
by Rev. George Parham. Sur. Robert Parham. p. 71.

9 March 1782. Micajah CAIN and Keziah Woodward. Sur. Isham Cain.
p. 29.

16 March 1784. Micajah CAIN and Elizabeth Wilkerson. Sur. Thomas
Wilkerson. p. 34.

21 February 1774. Peter CAIN and Judith Tucker, widow of Joel
Tucker. p. 18.

24 November 1785. Peter CAIN and Elizabeth Powell. Sur. Augustine
Claiborne. Wit: Hinchia Pettway. p. 40.

7 November 1793. Ruffin CAIN and Polly Whitehorn. Married 4
December by Rev. William Brown. Sur. Edward Whitehorn. p. 72.

5 September 1799. Thomas CAIN and Mary Malone. Returned 17
October by the Rev. Stith Parham. Sur. William Malone. p. 94.

26 February 1804. Joseph CANADY and Patty Jones. Married 29
February by Rev. Drewry Lane. Sur. John Jones. p. 114.

20 February 1808. James CANNADY and Elizabeth Scott. Married
21 February by Rev. Drewry Lane. Sur. Jordan Cannady. p. 128.

9 December 1806. John CANNADY and Creesy Chavis. Married by Rev.
Drewry Lane. Ministers' Returns p. 283.

6 April 1797. Joseph CANNON and Dorothy Vaughan, dau. Thomas
Vaughan. Married 8 April by Rev. Stith Parham. Sur. Thomas Hunt.
Wit: Fielding Vaughan. p. 86.

1 December 1762. John CARGILL and Sarah Avery, dau. Capt. Richard
Avery. Sur. Frederick Parker. p. 7.

15 September 1774. John CARGILL and Ann Eldridge, widow of William
Eldridge. Sur. Augustine Claiborne. p. 19.

22 October 1798. John CARGILL and Margaret Belsches. Sur. James
Raines Mason. p. 91.

27 August 1806. Nathaniel CARGILL and Mary E. Harrison. Sur.
William Harrison, Jr. p. 121.

9 September 1790. William Carter CARLOS and Patsey Vines, ward
of Green Hill, consent of Archelaus Carlos for William. Married
by the Rev. George Parham. Sur. Claiborne Cain. p. 61.

21 February 1782. Micajah CARREL and Elizabeth Andrews, dau.
Lydia Andrews. Micjah son of William and Ann Carrel. Sur. Stephen
Andrews. Wit: Richard Andrews and Susanna Andrews. p. 29.

9 February 1809. Henry W. CARRELL and Patsy Hix. Henry son of
Mark Carrell. Married 14 February by Rev. Drewry Lane. Sur.
William Carrell. p. 132.

31 October 1791. Mark CARRELL and Agatha Atkinson. Sur. Benjamin
Atkinson. p. 64.

3 November 1800. Hartwell CARSELEY and Sally Chappell. Sur.
James Chappell. p. 98.

6 December 1798. Crawford CARTER and Jincy Lewis. Sur. Richard
Madling. p. 92.

21 July 1785. Harris CARTER and Mary Butler, widow of Thomas
Butler. (Nee Norris, underage in 1765). Sur. John Carter. p. 38.

20 December 1786. Harris CARTER and Sally Walter Butler, dau.
Thomas Butler, deceased. Sur. John Carter, Sr. Wit: John Carter,
Jr. p. 45.

9 May 1785. John CARTER and Ursula Pennington, widow of David Pennington. Married 17 May by the Rev. John Cameron of Bristol Parish. Sur. John Cocke. p. 37.

7 December 1797. John CARTER and Elizabeth Mitchell. Sur. Benjamin Bailey. Wit: Lidey & Lucy Mitchell. p. 87.

31 December 1810. Richard CARTER and Lucy Davis, dau. Lucy Davis. Sur. Charles Davis. p. 138.

5 November 1795. Miles CARY and Elizabeth Yates. Sur. Robert Goodwin. Wit: Sally Booth. p. 78.

17 February 1775. Henry CATON and Elizabeth Wyche, widow of Benjamin Wyche. Sur. William Hines. p. 20.

25 October 1782. William CAUDELL and Larana Jones. Sur. John Jones. p. 31.

1 December 1808. Henry CHAMBLISS and Sally Parham. Married 22 December by Rev. James Rogers. p. 130.

11 April 1774. James CHAMBLISS and Sarah Moore, dau. Thomas Moore, deceased, and ward of David Graves. p. 18.

13 May 1782. Nathaniel CHAMBLISS and Mary Green. Married by the Rev. John Meglamore. Ministers' Returns p. 257.

5 March 1790. Theodorick CHAMBLISS and Nancy Oliver, dau. William Oliver. Sur. Jesse Peebles. Wit: Nathaniel and William Chambliss. p. 59.

23 February 1793. Thomas CHAMBLISS and Sally Graves. Married 28 February by Rev. Henry Moss. Sur. David Graves. p. 70.

27 March 1782. William CHAMBLISS and Rebecca Graves, dau. Solomon Graves. Sur. James Chambliss. Wit: John Graves and Thomas Chambliss. p. 30.

4 January 1802. Samuel CHAMPION and Elizabeth Wren. Sur. William Clanton. p. 104.

3 May 1804. William CHAMPION and Elizabeth Chambliss, dau. Nathaniel Chambliss. Sur. John Holt. p. 114.

11 April 1796. Benjamin CHAPPELL and Sally Porch. Married 14 April by Rev. Henry Moss. Sur. John Smith. p. 82.

1 January 1801. Benjamin CHAPPELL and Sarah Redding. Sur. Joel Redding. p. 100.

2 January 1806. Briggs CHAPPELL and Susan Jones. Sur. John Cross. p. 119.

5 November 1779. Henry CHAPPELL and Elizabeth Rives, dau. Elizabeth Rives who writes consent. Sur. Timothy Rives. Wit: Nathaniel Rives and Rebecca Mason. p. 25.

18 November 1799. Henry CHAPPELL and Rebecca Watkins Land. "Married Tuesday, the 19th" by the Rev. Drewry Lane. Sur. John Chappell. p. 94.

10 December 1808. Henry CHAPPELL and Nancy Little. Married 15 December by Rev. Drewry Lane. p. 130.

20 April 1769. James CHAPPELL and Sally Hines, dau. William Hines. James son of James Chappell, Sr. Sur. Jehu Barker (or Hugh Barker). p. 13.

25 May 1808. James CHAPPELL, Jr. and Polly Sturdivant. Married 26 May by Rev. James Rogers. Sur. Gilliam Harrup. Wit: Brent Fennel. p. 128.

17 March 1758. John CHAPPELL and Mary Hines, dau. Thomas Hines who is surety. p. 4.

10 October 1783. John CHAPPELL and Mary Edmunds. Married by the Rev. John Meglamore. Ministers' Returns p. 322.

3 February 1802. Littleberry CHAPPELL and Claramond Dobie. Married 4 February by Rev. Drewry Lane. Sur. Nathaniel Dobie. p. 105.

20 August 1772. Thomas CHAPPELL and Elizabeth Malone, infant (under age). Sur. Daniel Malone. Wit: Michael Malone. p. 15.

6 July 1801. Thomas CHAPPELL and Pamelia Chappell, dau. Elizabeth Chappell. Married 9 July by Rev. Drewry Lane. Sur. John Chappell. p. 101.

13 March 1789. William CHAPPELL and Lydia Leath. Married 20 March by Rev. John Meglamore. Sur. Nathaniel Dobie. p. 55.

23 February 1793. William CHAPPELL and Sally Kenniburgh, dau. John Kenniburgh. Married 26 February by Rev. Drewry Lane. Sur. Donaldson Potter. p. 71.

24 December 1803. William CHAPPELL and Sarah Fowler. Sur. William Wilborne. p. 113.

5 July 1804. William CHAPPELL and Patsy Bonner. Sur. John Bonner, Jr. p. 115.

17 August 1799. David CHARITY and Nancy Debberick. David Charity of Surry County. Married 18 August by Rev. Drewry Lane. Sur. Jones Canida. p. 93.

21 December 1799. Edward CHAVERS and Mary Cannaday, dau. Hew Cannaday. Married 22 December by Rev. Drewry Lane. Sur. John Canida. p. 95.

13 December 1788. James CHEATHAM and Anne Ellis, dau. Caleb Ellis. Sur. William Ellis. p. 53.

3 November 1769. Eldridge CLACK and Betty Hunt, dau. John Hunt, deceased. Sur. John Peters. p. 13.

20 December 1791. Matthew M. CLAIBORNE and Ann Carter Harrison, dau. Charles Harrison. Sur. Richard Claiborne. p. 65.

21 July 1791. John CLANTON and Rebecca Hearn. Sur. William Clanton. p. 63.

5 April 1784. Nathaniel CLANTON and Elizabeth Williamson. Sur. Buckner Lanier. p. 35.

28 March 1786. William CLANTON and Nancy Wrenn, consent of William Stuart. Sur. David Renn (Wrenn). Wit: Richard Rose and Mary Rose. p. 42.

1 April 1797. William CLANTON and Agnes Long. Sur. David Long. p. 85.

31 December 1788. Leonard CLARK and Susannah Capps, dau. Caleb Capps. Married 1 January 1789 by Rev. John Meglamore. Sur. William Smith. p. 53.

17 February 1796. Littleberry CLARK and Sally Lashly, consent of Robert Jones. Sur. William Clark. Married 19 February by Rev. Drewry Lane who says Lashby. p. 80.

8 December 1796. Richard CLARK and Milley Underhill. Married 11 December by Rev. Henry Moss. Sur. Benjamin Gary. p. 84.

6 December 1798. Richard CLARK and Susanna Wilkerson. Sur. Henry Wilkerson. Married by Rev. Augustine Heath. p. 92.

6 November 1800. Richard CLARK and Rosy Edwards. Sur. Henry Wilkerson. p. 98.

22 December 1786. Thomas CLARK and Lucy Hobbs. Married 26 December by Rev. John Meglamore. Sur. Frederick Hobbs. p. 45.

30 December 1795. William CLARK and Sarah Johnson. Sur. Carter Gilliam. p. 79.

6 December 1799. Willie CLARK and Lucy Holt, dau. Nathaniel Holt. Sur. John Holt. p. 95.

23 February 1807. Benjamin CLARY and Sally Lamb. Married 26 February by Rev. Drewry Lane. Sur. Benjamin Atkins. p. 124.

13 January 1794. Thomas CLARY and Jenney Presson. Sur. Richard Presson. p. 73.

23 January 1809. William CLARY and Elizabeth Cole. Married 26 January by Rev. Drewry Lane. Sur. William B. Cole. p. 131.

13 October 1806. Jesse CLAUD and Jincy Holt. Sur. Charles Holt. Married 23 October by Rev. James Rogers who says Nancy. p. 122.

22 September 1794. Francis CLEMENTS and Rebecca Parker, dau. Mary Parker. Sur. Robert Goodwyn. Wit: Henry Parker. p. 74.

21 September 1776. John COCKE and Lucy Herbert Claiborne, dau. Col. Augustine Claiborne. Sur. Buller Claiborne. Wit: Augustine Claiborne, Jr. p. 21.

27 December 1773. Lemuel COCKE and Ann Irby, ward of Richard Blunt. p. 18.

19 November 1768. Richard COCKE and Ann Claiborne, dau. Col. Augustine Claiborne. Richard son of Richard Cocke who consents. Sur. Herbert Claiborne. Wit: Nathaniel Cocke and William Warren. p. 12.

25 April 1807. Richard COCKE and Jane Bland Ruffin, dau. Thomas B. Ruffin. Richard Cocke of Surry County. Sur. Thomas Blunt, Jr. Wit: James Atkinson and Archibald Atkinson. p. 125.

7 August 1783. James Wilson COKER and Martha Jones, dau. Nathaniel Jones. Sur. Richard Bailey. p. 33.

1 February 1803. James COKER and Lucy White. Married 3 February by Rev. Drewry Lane. Sur. Anthony Andrews. p. 110.

28 January 1807. Jonathan COKER and Diza White. Married 29 January by Rev. Drewry Lane. Sur. James Coker. p. 123.

19 February 1802. John B. COLE and Ruinah Avent, consent of Rebekah Avent. Married 25 February by Rev. Robert Murrell, Sr. of Southampton Co. Sur. Thomas Avent. p. 105.

5 April 1804. William B. COLE and Nancy Hancock, dau. Elizabeth Hancock. Married 17 May by Rev. Drewry Lane. Sur. Stephen Rogers. p. 114.

8 May 1792. Benjamin COLLIER and Winnifred Gilliam, consent of John Mason. Sur. Walter Gilliam. p. 67.

27 January 1759. Charles COLLIER and Susanna Smith, age 21, dau. of William Smith, deceased and sister of Joseph Smith, who consents. Sur. Josiah Smith. p. 4.

22 December 1801. Richard COLLIER and Dilley Coker. Married 24 December by Rev. Drewry Lane. Sur. George Hines. p. 104.

18

21 December 1780. Sampson COLLIER and Sarah Gilliam, widow. Sur. Peter Jones. Wit: Henry Gee. p. 27.

4 June 1795. Isaac COLLIER and Lucy Hewett, dau. Elizabeth Hewett. Sur. William Price Walker. p. 77.

3 January 1805. William COLLIER and Elizabeth J. Robertson. Sur. Allen Cain. p. 116.

23 March 1788. James COOK and Elizabeth Lamb, dau. William Lamb. James Cook of York County. Sur. John Lamb, Jr. p. 51.

3 August 1797. James COOK and Rebecca Wilkerson. Sur. Nathan Wilkerson. p. 85.

27 May 1802. John COOK and Elizabeth Cotton, ward of Richard Gary. Married 3 June by Rev. Drewry Lane. Sur. Cary Cotton. Wit: John Finch. p. 107.

18 September 1797. Richard COOK and Deidama Cotton. Sur. William Porch. p. 85.

9 January 1800. Edwin COOPER and Elizabeth Gilliam. Sur. Howell Cooper. Wit: W. Stuart. p. 96.

5 December 1799. Frederick COOPER and Elizabeth Barker. Married 12 December by Rev. William Hargrave. Sur. Archibald W. Bowles. p. 95.

17 March 1788. John COOPER and Caty Stacy, consent of Sarah Stacy. Sur. James Johnson. p. 50.

9 February 1795. John C. COOPER and Polly Avent, dau. Thomas Avent. Married 15 February by Rev. Robert Murrell, Sr. Sur. Carter Gilliam. p. 76.

7 June 1804. Thomas COOPER and Polly Birdsong. Sur. Nicholas Morris, Sr. Married by Rev. Drewry Lane. p. 115.

1 May 1783. Jacob CORNWALL and Sarah Wilkinson. Jacob Cornwall of Southampton County. Sur. William Bailey. p. 33.

2 July 1787. Archibald COTTON and Caty Hill. Married 7 July by Rev. John Meglamore. Sur. Henry Jarrad. p. 47.

11 December 1792. Cary COTTON and Nancy Harrison. Sur. William Harrison. p. 69.

28 January 1809. Frederick COTTON and Polly Christian. Married 1 February by Rev. Drewry Lane. Sur. Charles Christian. p. 131.

18 August 1789. Hardy COTTON and Patty Saunders. Sur. John Saunders. p. 56.

20 December 1793. Charles COTTRELL and Milly Sears. Married
21 December by Rev. Drewry Lane. Sur. Peter Bailey. p. 73.

26 August 1792. Phillip COX and Elizabeth Gibbons. Sur. Lawrence
Gibbons. Wit: Ann Gibbons. p. 67.

6 November 1795. William CREEDLE and Sally Felts. Married 7
November by Rev. Drewry Lane. Sur. Jesse Felts. Wit: Benjamin B.
Rosser. p. 78.

15 March 1787. John CRO_S and Lucy Tomlinson. Sur. Miles Birdsong.
p. 46.

18 December 1780. William CROSS and Rebekah Wallace. Sur. Jesse
Wallace. p. 27.

10 February 1778. Christopher CROSSLAND and ------ -------
Sur. Robert Lewis. p. 24.

2 December 1786. Shadrock CROWDER and Lilly Ambros, dau. Thomas
Ambros. Sur. Joel Redding. Wit: John Redding and George Booth,
Jr. Married 17 December by Rev. Jesse Lee. p. 44.

14 December 1793. Hezekiah CURTIS and Sally Murdock, consent of
Matthew Parham. Sur. Allen Sturdivant. Wit: John Green. p.73.

3 November 1808. Littleberry CURTIS and Gincy Owen. Married 30
November by Rev. James Rogers. Sur. James Welborne. p. 129.

7 April 1796. William DARCHESTER and Elizabeth Scoggin. Sur.
William Scoggin. p. 82. See William Dorchester.

28 September 1792. John DAVIS and Nancy Smith Whittington.
Married by Rev. William Brown. Ministers' Returns p. 267.

22 December 1801. John DAVIS and Peggy Coker. Married 24 December
by Rev. Drewry Lane. Sur. George Hines. p. 104.

26 February 1798. Josiah DAVIS and Sarah Edwards. Married 27
February by Rev. Drewry Lane. p. 89.

16 December 1784. Marriot DAVIS and Mary Nicholson, dau. Michael
Nicholson, deceased. Sur. Walter Bailey. p. 36.

20 May 1796. Matthew DAVIS and Sally Gilbert. Sur. Edward
Whitehorn. p. 82.

16 September 1788. Thomas DAVIS and Creasy Cain. Sur. Robert
Watson. Married by the Rev. John Meglamore. p. 52.

22 November 1810. William DAVIS and Rebecca Blow. Married 28
November by Rev. Drewry Lane. Sur. John Davis. p. 137.

7 February 1797. Major DEBRICK and Silvey Cannady, consent of
Hew Cannady (Hugh?). Major Debrick of Surry County. Married
9 February by Rev. Drewry Lane. Sur. Joseph Cannady. p. 82.

25 October 1759. Joseph DENNIS and Lucretia Parham, infant
(under age) dau. Matthew Parham. Sur. Thomas Young. p. 5.

7 May 1789. Richard DENNIS and Drada Hartley. Sur. Joseph Dinnis.
Wit: William Goodfair. Returned October 1789 by Rev. George
Parham. p. 55.

13 April 1803. David DENSON and Peggy Wade. Married 15 April
by Rev. Drewry Lane. Sur. Hardy Adkins. p. 110.

15 April 1784. John DENTON and Peggy Creagh. Sur. John Moss.
p. 35.

24 October 1797. George DILLARD and Nancy E. Tomlinson. Sur.
James Bailey. p. 87.

14 June 1804. Richmond DILLARD and Sally Andrews, ward of
S. Boykin. Sur. Anthony Copeland. p. 115.

21 May 1767. Frederick DIXON and Nanny Hines, dau. William Hines.
Sur. Henry Dixon. p. 11.

16 November 1789. Tilman DIXON and Mary Carlos, dau. Archelaus
Carlos. Sur. Robert Booth. p. 57.

20 April 1803. William DOBIE and Polly Chappell. Married 21
April by Rev. Drewry Lane. Sur. James Chappell. p. 111.

17 July 1805. William DOBIE and Dolly Niblett, dau. Sterling
Niblett. Married 25 July by Rev. James Rogers. Sur. Nathaniel
Dobie. p. 118.

17 April 1796. William DORCHESTER and Elizabeth Coggin. Married
by Rev. Henry Moss. Ministers' Returns p. 271. See William
Darchester.

22 December 1790. George DOWDY and Susanna Owen. Sur. Ransom
Stokes. p. 62.

8 July 1807. Robert DOWNMAN and Lucy M. Mason, dau. John R.
Mason. Sur. Benjamin Wyche. p. 125.

10 January 1810. Elias DOYEL and Willy Bailey. Sur. Thomas
Bayley. p. 135.

7 November 1793. Newett DREW and Lucy Smith, dau. Isham Smith.
Sur. Joshua Claud. Married by Rev. William Brown. p. 72.

6 November 1788. Richard DREWRY and Nancy Murray Harwood, dau.
John Harwood. Sur. James Drewry. Wit: Thomas Flowers and Michael
Bailey. p. 53.

3 September 1793. James DRURY and Molly Avent, dau. John Avent. Sur. Fortunatus Jarrett. p. 71.

11 June 1785. Richard DUELL and Jinsey Sanders. Sur. John Sanders. p. 38.

2 November 1782. Drury DUNN and Martha Powell, dau. Edward Powell, Sr. Sur. Peter Raney. p. 31.

21 August 1788. James DUNN and Amey Rollings. Sur. David Ivey. p. 51.

4 March 1806. John DUNN and Susan Rochell. Married 7 March by Rev. James Rogers. Sur. James Rochell. Wit: John Newby. p. 120.

10 February 1769. Nathaniel DUNN and Rebecca Parham, sister William Parham. Sur. Herbert Claiborne. Wit: Nathaniel Parham and Robert W. Raines. p. 12.

3 November 1791. Osmond DUNN and Silvia Hubbard. Sur. Groves Sammons. Wit: James Sammons. Married by Rev. William Brown. p. 64.

25 June 1772. Thomas DUNN and Sarah Hobbs, dau. Thomas Hobbs, deceased, and Sarah Hobbs. Sur. Frederick Hobbs. Wit: William Tomlinson and James Mason. p. 15.

29 June 1807. Thomas DUNN and Betsey Cureton. Married 1 July by Rev. James Rogers. Sur. Howell Adkins. Wit: John Beddingfield. p. 125.

20 December 1802. William DUNN and Celia Rainey. Sur. Peter Rainey. p. 109.

1 December 1800. William ECKLES and Polly Bobbitt. Sur. John Bobbitt. p. 99.

13 May 1805. William ECHOLS and Martha Hamlin Vincent. Sur. Robert Pettway. p. 117.

19 August 1757. Henry EDMUNDS and Sarah Briggs of Surry County. Henry Edmunds of St. Andrew's Parish, Brunswick County. Sur. Richard Stark. p. 3.

13 January 1755. Nicholas EDMUNDS and Mary Nicholson, widow. Sur. John Irby. p. 1.

4 June 1787. Benjamin EDWARDS and Temperance Peters. Sur. John Mason. p. 47.

21 November 1767. Edward EDWARDS and Beea Brockwell. Edward Edwards of George County. Sur. Augustine Claiborne. Wit: Isham Cotton and Charles Love. p. 11.

15 April 1802. Gordan EDWARDS and Nancy Prince. Married by Rev. James Rogers. Ministers' Returns p. 278. See Jordan Edwards.

16 February 1786. John EDWARDS and Temperance Parker. Sur. John Pettus. Wit: Buckner Lanier. p. 41.

1 April 1802. Jordan EDWARDS and Nancy Prince. Sur. Joseph Prince. Wit: David Williams. p. 106. See Gordan Edwards.

6 December 1804. Jordan EDWARDS and Polly C. Weathers. Married 27 December by Rev. James Rogers. Sur. Nathan Weathers. p. 116.

22 December 1794. Joseph EDWARDS and Ann Sikes. Sur. Harris Cotton. Wit: Benjamin Johnson. p. 75.

3 August 1787. Thomas EDWARDS and Milly Blizzard, dau. Samuel Blizzard. Sur. Robert Bailey. p. 47.

5 September 1805. Thomas EDWARDS and Lucy Jones. Married by Rev. Drewry Lane. Ministers' Returns p. 280.

20 July 1756. William EDWARDS and Sarah Edmunds, dau. of Thomas Edmunds, deceased, and sister of J. Edmunds. William Edwards of Brunswick County. Sur. William Eldridge. Wit: Elizabeth Gray. p.2.

30 May 1774. William EDWARDS and Susanna Edmunds, dau. of John Edmunds, deceased. Sur. William Irby. p. 19.

7 November 1793. William EDWARDS and Patsy Underhill. Sur. Robert Ray. p. 72.

27 June 1801. William EDWARDS and Amey Jefferson. Sur. Robert Ray. p. 101.

21 August 1790. Thomas ELDRIDGE and Susanna H. Massenburg, consent of John Massenburg. Sur. James Bailey. p. 60.

22 August 1804. Thomas ELDRIDGE and Elizabeth Hall. Married 23 August by Rev. James Rogers. Sur. Nathaniel Cargill. p. 115.

5 November 1798. Boling ELLIS and Polly Cole, dau. Mrs. Elizabeth Holdsworth. Married 15 November by Rev. Drewry Lane. Sur. Wyatt Sharp. p. 91.

23 January 1788. Caleb ELLIS and Mary Gilbert. Married 24 January by Rev. John Meglamore. Sur. James Gilbert. p. 50.

23 December 1786. Ephraim ELLIS and Jane Heath, dau. Margaret Heath. Married 25 December by Rev. Jesse Lee. Sur. John Chappell. Wit: William Heath. p. 45.

1 June 1781. Isaac ELLIS and Cherry Sharp, dau. John Sharp, deceased. Sur. John Ellis. p. 28.

30 January 1781. John ELLIS and Edy Carrel, consent of William Carrel, consent of William Ellis who is surety. Wit: Richard Andrews and Harwood Birt. p. 27.

25 May 1799. John ELLIS and Sally Underhill. Sur. Seth Mason. p. 93.

16 December 1786. Micah (Micajah) ELLIS and Elizabeth Wright, ward of William Ellis who is surety. Wit: Stephen Andrews. p. 45.

22 December 1774. Richard ELLIS and Elizabeth Sharp, age 22, dau. of John Sharp, deceased. Sur. Burwell Sharp. p. 19.

25 November 1799. Robert ELLIS and Nancy Barker. Married 28 November by Rev. William Brown. Sur. Richard Hargrave. p. 94.

18 April 1780. Thomas ELLIS and Amery (Amy) Saunders, dau. John Saunders who is surety. p. 26.

1 November 1783. William ELLIS, Jr. and Martha Ellis, consent of Caleb Ellis, and William Ellis. Sur. Isaac Ellis. Wit: Stephen Andress. p. 33.

28 August 1795. Wright ELLIS and Sally Andrews. Sur. Stephen Andrews. Wit: Nancy and Susanna Andrews. Returned 1 October by Rev. Drewry Lane. p. 78.

5 December 1793. Wyatt ELLIS and Mary Ellis. Married 19 December by Rev. Drewry Lane. Sur. Benjamin Ellis. p. 72.

14 April 1787. Thomas EMARY and Keziah Bishop. Sur. George Salomon. Wit: Lewis Salomon, p. 47.

14 December 1789. Francis EPPES and Sally Winfield, dau. Robert Winfield. Sur. Henry Winfield. Returned February 1790 by the Rev. George Parham. p. 58.

1 October 1774. Joel EPPES and Lucy Meachum, dau. Banks Meachum. Sur. John Baird. p. 19.

16 April 1804. John P. EPPES and Nancy Willcox. Married 3 May by Rev. Joseph Hill. Sur. William Parsons. Wit: Lucretia Ellis. P. 114.

7 May 1789. Thomas EPPES and Sally Winfield. Sur. John Huson. p. 55.

5 November 1804. Thomas EPPES and Elizabeth M. Randolph. Sur. Ruffin Cain. Wit: John Parham. p. 116.

21 April 1769. Thomas ESKRIDGE and Elizabeth Pennington, widow. Sur. John Walker. Wit: John Hamlin. p. 13.

17 February 1792. Anthony EVANS and Susanna Chappell, dau. Howell Chappell. Married 19 February by Rev. Daniel Southall. Sur. Thomas Travis. p. 66.

6 April 1786. Benjamin EVANS and Mary Ellis, dau. William Ellis. Sur. Waller Bailey. Wit: Robert Bailey. p. 42.

15 December 1800. Benjamin EVANS and Rebecca Porch. Married 16 December by Rev. Drewry Lane. Sur. Anthony Evans. Wit: Henry Porch and John Pennington. p. 99.

31 March 1798. Etheldred EVANS and Selah Davis, dau. Etheldred Davis. Married 1 April by Rev. Drewry Lane. Sur. William Wrenn. p. 89.

1 March 1798. Jesse EVANS and Sally Roe. Married 2 March by Rev. Henry Moss. Sur. Benjamin Evans, Jr. p. 89.

10 March 1809. William EVANS and Lucy Sturdivant. Sur. Thomas Sturdivant. Married by the Rev. James Rogers. p. 132.

27 January 1792. Robert EZELL and Rebecca Thweats. Sur. Jesse Ezell. Married by Rev. William Brown. p. 66.

14 February 1795. Zacheus EZELL and Silvia Underwood. Sur. Cain Underwood. p. 76.

31 January 1775. Enoch FAGAN and Ruiana Judkins, age 23, dau. Mary Judkins. Sur. Gray Judkins. p. 20.

18 January 1792. Edward FAISON and Charlotte Jones. Married 19 January by Rev. Henry Moss. Sur. Robert Smith. p. 66.

17 January 1799. Lawrence FAISON and Cherry Holloway. Married 22 January by Rev. Drewry Lane. Sur. Job Holloway. p. 92.

8 February 1803. Thomas FAISON and Avey White, consent of James White who is surety. Married 17 February by Rev. Drewry Lane who says Avery. p. 110.

18 December 1790. Augustine FELTS and Phebe Rose. Married 21 December by Rev. John Mason. Sur. Richard Rose. p. 62.

15 September 1785. Bolling FELTS and Mary Felts. Sur. George Rives. p. 38.

22 May 1798. Gray FELTS and Rebecca Magee. Sur. Robert Magee. p. 90.

6 January 1792. Henry FELTS and Mary Magee, dau. Drury Magee, Sr. Sur. William Felts. p. 66.

31 December 1788. Jesse FELTS and Cherry Hix. Sur. Thomas Hicks. Wit: James E. Bailey. p. 53.

2 October 1800. Kinchen FELTS and Polly Harwood. Sur. Phillip Williams. p. 98.

17 August 1781. Nathan FELTS and Sally Hargrave. Sur. Nathaniel Felts. p. 28.

5 January 1788. Bryan FENNEL and Permely Hobbs, dau. Joseph Hobbs. Sur. Stephen Hobbs. Married 11 January by Rev. Jesse Lee who says Bryant Fennel. p. 49.

29 December 1796. William FINCH and Polly Barker. Sur. Hansel Sammons. p. 85.

, February 1792. James FLETCHER and Mary Jones. Sur. James Jones. p. 66.

2 January 1790. John FLETCHER and Rebecca Wyche, dau. Mary Whche. Sur. Nathaniel Wyche. Wit: Anne Goodwyn. p. 58.

17 September 1792. Thomas FLETCHER and Elizabeth Cain. Married 20 September by Rev. William Brown. Sur. Carter Gilliam. Wit: George Stegal. p. 68.

22 January 1789. Absalom FLOWERS and Betsy Johnson. Sur. Carter Gilliam. p. 54.

5 August 1790. Benjamin FLOWERS and Anne Owen. Sur. John Bonner. Married by Rev. George Parham. p. 60.

11 May 1756. John FORD and Olive Tharp, dau. Joseph Tharp who is surety. p. 2.

7 February 1758. Joshua FORT and Mary Celia Tharp, dau. Joseph Tharp. Joshua of Southhampton County and ward of Arthur Foster. Sur. Major Tiller. Wit: John Tiller, James Milner, Benjamin Barham and Cornelius Mabry. p. 3.

25 April 1796. William FOWLER and Sally Oliver. Married by Rev. Stith Parham. Sur. Gabriel Moss. p. 82.

6 August 1789. Balaam FREEMAN and Polly Graves. Sur. David Graves. Married 13 August by Rev. Henry Moss. p. 56.

2 August 1798. Balaam FREEMAN and Mary Jones. Returned 25 October by Rev. Stith Parham. Sur. Anthony Mason. p. 91.

23 December 1788. Henry FREEMAN and Elizabeth Roe. Married 25 December by Rev. John Meglamore. Sur. John Magee. p. 53.

15 August 1798. James FREEMAN and Patsey Freeman. Returned 25 September by Rev. Drewry Lane. Sur. Littleberry Jennings. p. 91.

5 February 1801. James FREEDMAN and Jincy Whitehorn. Sur. John Green. p. 100.

21 June 1757. Joel FREEMAN and Patty Richardson, dau. William Richardson, deceased. Sur. William Richardson. p. 3.

3 February 1803. Josiah FREEMAN and Jenny Hart. Married 19 February by Rev. Drewry Lane. Sur. Robert Hart. p. 110.

13 December 1781. William FREEMAN and Ann Judkins. Sur. Joseph Birdsong. p. 29.

15 January 1789. Benjamin GARY and Mary Underhill. Sur. William Underhill. p. 54.

6 May 1802. Gray GARY and Mary B. Fowler, ward of Thomas Chappell. Married 20 May by Rev. Stith Parham. Sur. William Malone. Wit: John Ramey, Henry Gary and James Anderson. p. 106.

4 March 1786. John GARY and Sally Weaver, dau. Henry Weaver. Married 5 March by Rev. John Cameron. Sur. William Gary. Wit: John Hamlin. p. 42.

1 January 1795. Richard GARY and Lucy Malone. Sur. Jones Bonner. p. 75.

15 August 1765. William GARY, Jr. and Boyce Gee. Sur. William Heath, Jr. p. 9.

27 August 1783. William GARY and Lucy Weaver, dau. Henry Weaver who is surety. p. 33.

26 December 1791. George GAULL and Lucretia Davis, dau. John Davis. Sur. Thomas Fletcher. Wit: Isaac Vines Collier. Married by Rev. William Brown. p. 65.

20 December 1793. Edmund GAY and Nancy Wakefield. Returned 2 January 1794, by Rev. Drewry Lane. Sur. Peter Bailey. p. 73.

22 January 1787. Simon GAY and Mary Freeman. Sur. William Brittle. p. 46.

17 December 1807. Simon GAY and Anna Freeman. Sur. Edmund Gay. p. 126.

18 March 1773. Chappell GEE and Rebecca Lucas, dau. William Lucas, deceased. Sur. William Mason. p. 17.

6 December 1787. Charles GEE and Susannah Peebles (under age), dau. Mary Peebles. Sur. John Peebles. Wit: E. Butler and Martha Cleveland. p. 48.

16 March 1759. Henry GEE and Frances Parham, dau. Ephraim Parham who is surety. p. 4.

13 January 1803. Henry GEE and Sally Felts. Married 20 January by Rev. Drewry Lane. Sur. Robert Dudley. Wit: Jane Mason. p. 109.

28 February 1793. Birrel GENNANS and Anna Rogers (Burwell Jennings?) Married by Rev. Henry Ross. Ministers' Returns p. 267.

23 February 1795. Frederick GEORGE and Lettuce Hargrave. Married 26 February by Rev. Drewry Lane. Sur. Jesse Evans. p. 76.

5 May 1802. John GEORGE and Susanna Carrell. Returned 3 June by Rev. Drewry Lane. Sur. William Carrell. p. 106.

17 March 1768. Lawrence GIBBONS, Jr. and Lucy Jones, dau. James Jones. Sur. William Hines. p. 11.

12 June 1781. William GILBERT and Susanna Moss, dau. Henry Moss, Sr. Sur. Ephraim Moss. p. 28.

6 September 1798. Zachariah GILBERT and Polly Andrews. Sur. Edwin Long. p. 91.

27 August 1800. Anselm GILLIAM and Sarah Clark. Sur. Ambrose Andrews. p. 98.

4 February 1792. Benjamin Dunn GILLIAM and Lucy Loftin. Sur. William Loftin. Married by Rev. William Brown. p. 66.

23 December 1805. Burwell GILLIAM and Mary Ann Miller. Married 25 December by Rev. James Rogers. Sur. John Holt. p. 119.

19 July 1782. Carter GILLIAM and Elizabeth Hancock, dau. Rebecka Hancock. Carter son of Anselm Gilliam. Sur. John Carter. Wit: Benjamin Lanier, Levy Rochell and Jesse Wren. p. 30.

20 March 1788. Charles GILLIAM and Mary Manny. Married 3 April by Rev. John Meglamore who says Maning. Sur. Anselm Gilliam. p. 50.

5 February 1795. Gray GILLIAM and Elizabeth Stuart. Sur. Stephen Temple. Wit: Matthew Lee. p. 76.

5 December 1805. James GILLIAM and Elizabeth Magee. Married 12 December by Rev. James Rogers. p. 119.

26 February 1787. Jordan GILLIAM and Anne Betts, dau. Banaster Betts. Returned 29 March by Rev. John Meglamore. Sur. James Jones. Wit: Drury Betts. p. 46.

16 August 1787. Samuel GILLIAM and Patsy Hunt, dau. Thomas Hunt. Sur. Dixon Hall. Wit: Charles Gilliam. p. 48.

19 May 1774. Thomas GILLIAM, Jr. and Sarah Williamson, dau. Arthur Williamson. Thomas Gilliam, Jr. of Southhampton County. p. 18.

7 January 1789. Thomas GILLIAM (age 84) and Selah Sorsby (age ca. 45). Sur. Frederick Loftin. p. 54.

27 September 1786. Walter GILLIAM and Elizabeth Barham. Samson and Mary Collier consent for Walter Gilliam. Sur. Jonathan Harrup. Wit: Drury Cooper. Married 5 October by Rev. John Meglamore. p.43.

5 January 1789. William GILLIAM and Cherry Tyus, dau. Benjamin Tyus. Sur. Howell Bosman. p. 54.

9 October 1792. William GLOVER and Susannah B. Roberts, dau. Sarah Roberts. Sur. John Bonner. p. 68.

25 August 1797. William GLOVER and Betty Sammons. Sur. James Shannon. p. 85.

20 October 1789. John GOLD and Abbey Andrews, dau. Henry Andrews who is surety. Wit: Roe and Willie Magee. Married 24 October by Rev. John Meglamore. p. 56.

20 December 1786. James GOLIGHTLY and Susanna Redding. Returned 6 January 1787 by Rev. Jesse Lee. Sur. Joel Redding. Wit: Androsen Redding. p. 45.

26 October 1803. William Camp GOODRICH and Martha Smith. Sur. William Chambliss. p. 112.

18 December 1788. James GOODRUM and Molly Hartley. Sur. Thomas Hartley. Married or returned 10 January 1789 by Rev. John Meglamore who says Polly. p. 53.

19 February 1784. Armistead GOODWYN and Ann Wyche, dau. Mary Wyche. Sur. Littleberry Mason. Wit: Mary Chapman Wyche and Sterling Tucker. p. 34.

28 August 1794. Joseph GOODWYN and Jane Robertson. Sur. Daniel Neves. p. 74.

26 September 1797. Robert GOODWYN and Susanna Mason, dau. Elizabeth Mason. Sur. Archer Parker. p. 85.

17 February 1785. Sampson GRANTHAM and Elizabeth Mansell Simmons, dau. Rebecca Simmons. Sampson Grantham of Surry County. Sur. John Grantham. Wit: Thomas Grantham and Francis Smith. Married by Rev. John Cameron of Bristol Parish. p. 37.

1 December 1780. John GRAVES and Sarah Parham, dau. Nathaniel Parham. Sur. Solomon Graves. Wit: Henry Gee and James Gee. p. 26.

21 August 1783. Richard GRAVES and Dolly Blunt, dau. Richard Blunt, deceased, and ward of William Blunt. Richard Graves of Dinwiddie County. Sur. William Mason. Wit: Lucretia Jones and Richard Blunt. p. 33.

22 April 1807. Solomon GRAVES and Polly Pennington, dau. Marcus Pennington. Married 29 April by Rev. James Rogers. Sur. Winfield Pennington. p. 125.

9 October 1758. Abraham GREEN and Ann Blunt, widow. Sur. John Irby. p. 4.

4 February 1808. Balaam GREEN and Lucy Owen. Sur. Joshua Owen. Married 2 March by Rev. James Rogers. p. 128.

7 December 1809. Balaam GREEN and Sarah B. Chappell, dau. Thomas Chappell. Sur. Samuel Owen. Wit: Robert Chappell, John Rainey and Lucretia Randolph. p. 134.

11 September 1786. Burwell GREEN and Elizabeth Hartley. Married 20 September by Rev. John Meglamore. Sur. Robert Jones. Wit: Joseph Hartley and Thomas Harley. p. 43.

28 August 1801. James GREEN and Elizabeth Moore, dau. Barram Moore. Sur. John Green. p. 102.

29 December 1806. John GREEN and Polly Adams, dau. Amos Adams. Married 30 December by Rev. James Rogers. Sur. Jesse Owen.p. 123.

2 January 1806. Thomas GREEN and Frances Smith. Married 15 January by Rev. James Rogers. Sur. John Bonner. p. 119.

16 September 1777. Richard GREGORY and Mary Broadnax, widow of William Broadnax. Richard son of Roger Gregory of Lunenburg County. p. 22.

31 August 1809. Burwell GRIGG and Mary Chambliss, dau. Nathaniel Chambliss. Married 6 September by Rev. James Rogers. Sur. Littleton Chambliss. p. 133.

27 December 1808. Mitchell GRIGG and Polly Chambliss, dau. William Chambliss, deceased, ward of Nathaniel Chambliss. Married 4 January 1809 by Rev. James Rogers. Sur. Smith Parham. p. 130.

24 July 1809. Richard B. GRIGG and Frances M. Chambliss, dau. Theoderick Chambliss. Married 26 July by Rev. James Rogers. Sur. Burwell Grigg. p. 133.

14 January 1786. Ambrose GRIZZARD and Edney Tilir. Married by Rev. John Melgamore. Ministers' Returns p. 258.

30 December 1805. Ambrose GRIZZARD and Lucy Pate. Married 1 January 1806 by Rev. James Rogers. Sur. Henry Pate. p. 119.

15 February 1800. William GRIZZARD and Milly Sledge. Sur. Henry Pate. p. 96.

23 November 1793. Newsom GWALTNEY and Mary Jones. Sur. Howell Jones. p. 72.

29 January 1802. Joel HAILS and Sarah Adams, dau. James Adams. Sur. Benjamin Adams. p. 105.

13 February 1789. Hubbard HALL and Frances Haddon Parham, dau. Abraham Parham. Sur. Thomas Parham. Married 26 February by Rev. Jesse Lee. p. 55.

19 January 1774. James HALL and Elizabeth Owen, widow. p. 18.

23 May 1787. Joel HALL and Betsy Chambliss, dau. James Chambliss. Sur. John Hall. p. 47.

17 April 1800. William HALL and Nancy Bailey. Sur. Benjamin W. Johnston. Married by Rev. William Hargrave. p. 96.

7 April 1807. Stephen HAMLIN and Eliza Felts. Married 9 April by Rev. Drewry Lane. Sur. James Briggs. p. 124.

18 November 1795. William HAMLIN and Elizabeth Bridges. Married 20 November by Rev. Drewry Lane. Sur. Joseph Rosser. p. 79.

18 April 1809. Jeremiah HANCOCK and Polly Cooper. Sur. Zachariah Hancock. p. 132.

20 July 1804. John HANCOCK and Rebecca Phillips. Married 21 July by Rev. Drewry Lane. Sur. Thomas Hancock. p. 115.

5 June 1802. Zachariah HANCOCK and Sally W. Cole, consent of Elizabeth Holdsworth. Sur. Boling Ellis. Married by Rev. Drewry Lane. p. 107.

8 November 1808. Henry S. HARDAWAY and Mary Gilliam, dau. Martha Gilliam. Sur. Robert Harper. p. 129.

14 February 1756. John HARDAWAY and Rebecca Pepper, dau. Richard Pepper. Sur. David Smith. p. 2.

22 July 1785. Thomas HARDAWAY and Rebekah Powell. Sur. Thomas Wilkinson. Wit: David Owen and John Wilborn. p. 38.

17 February 1792. Benjamin HARGRAVE and Sarah Holleman. Sur. John Hargrave. p. 66.

25 November 1791. John HARGRAVE and Elizabeth Smith, dau. Reker Smith. Sur. Benjamin Hargrave. p. 65.

25 November 1799. Richard HARGRAVE and Nancy Ellis, dau. Benjamin Ellis. Married 28 November by Rev. Drewry Lane. Sur. Robert Ellis. p. 94.

10 November 1810. Robert HARGRAVE and Polly Presson, dau. Nicholas Presson. Married 13 November by Rev. Drewry Lane. Sur. Joseph Jarrad. p. 137.

23 January 1790. Samuel HARGRAVE and Ann Holdsworth. Sur. Charles Holdsworth. p. 59.

18 November 1791. William HARGRAVE and Sally Ellis. Married 1 December by Rev. Drewry Lane. Sur. Benjamin Ellis, Jr. p. 65.

24 February 1787. Michael HAROD and Elizabeth Freeman, dau. John Freeman. Sur. William Wootton. Wit: George Bell. p. 46.

21 December 1782. William HARPER and Jane Bonner. Married by Rev. Jesse Lee. Ministers' Returns p. 322.

8 January 1801. Benjamin HARRIS and Rebecca Avent, dau. Rebekah Avent. Married 20 January by Rev. Robert Murrell, Sr. of South-hampton County. Sur. Thomas Avent. p. 100.

20 December 1808. James HARRIS and Frances Ellis, dau. John Ellis. James Harris of Surry County. Sur. Thomas Velvin. Wit: Matthew Booth. p. 130.

30 December 1774. Alexander HARRISON and Frances Hobbs, dau. Thomas Hobbs, deceased. Alexander son of Richard Harrison. Sur. Nathaniel Tomlinson. Wit: Frederick Heath and John Lessenberry. p. 20.

30 May 1806. Benjamin HARRISON and Frances Jackson, dau. Francis Jackson. Sur. Henry Hill. p. 121.

3 November 1791. Charles HARRISON and Martha Eppes. Married 17 November by Rev. Henry Moss. Sur. William Harrison. p. 64.

7 April 1796. Charles HARRISON and Polly Wilkerson. Married 21 April by Rev. Henry Moss. Sur. Henry Wilkerson. p. 82.

6 March 1806. Charles HARRISON and Polly Booth. Married 15 March by Rev. James Rogers. Sur. Marcus Pair. p. 120.

2 February 1809. Charles HARRISON and Patsy Porch. Married 4 February by Rev. James Rogers. p. 131.

27 September 1758. Henry HARRISON, Gent., and Elizabeth Avery, dau. Capt. Richard Avery. Sur. Augustine Claiborne. p. 4.

4 February 1791. Henry HARRISON and Elizabeth Underhill. Sur. Howell Underhill. p. 62.

2 April 1793. Henry HARRISON and Peggy Moss, consent of Joshua Moss. Sur. Alfred Moss. p. 71.

4 October 1798. Henry HARRISON and Mary Baird. Married 8 October by Rev. Drewry Lane. Sur. Hamlin Baird and Charles Baird. p. 91.

23 December 1782. John HARRISON and Patty Winfield. Married by Rev. Jesse Lee. Minister's Returns p. 322.

28 December 1786. John HARRISON and Fanny Winfield, dau. William and Elizabeth Winfield. Sur. Thomas Wilkerson. Wit: James Lee. Married by Rev. John Meglamore. p. 45.

27 March 1798. John HARRISON and Elizabeth Redding. Sur. Joel Eckols. p. 89.

2 March 1786. Josiah HARRISON and Mary Underhill. Married 4 March by Rev. John Cameron of Bristol Parish. Sur. Howell Underhill. p. 42.

20 February 1798. Josiah HARRISON and Frances Ray. Married 22 February by Rev. Drewry Lane. Sur. Charles Mitchell. p. 89.

7 August 1775. Lemuel HARRISON and Susanna Eppes, dau. Edward Eppes. Lemuel Harrison of Prince George County. Sur. Benjamin Baird. Wit: Sarah Tomlinson. p. 21.

18 February 1775. Peter Cole HARRISON and Margaret Hay, dau. John Hay, deceased, and Judith Hay, born 5 November 1751, signed William Willie, Rector. Nathaniel Harrison writes that Peter Cole Harrison is 21 on 18 February 1775. Sur. Hamilton Jones. Wit: Hannah Harrison and Frederick Jones. p. 20.

29 May 1797. Richard HARRISON and Elizabeth Adkins. Married 2 June by Rev. Henry Moss. Sur. Richard Cook. p. 85.

27 March 1801. Richard HARRISON and Polly Felts. Married 2 April by the Rev. Drewry Lane. Sur. Cary Cotton. p. 100.

23 April 1767. Thomas HARRISON and Mary Jenkins, widow. Thomas Harrison of Brunswick County. Sur. William Tomlinson. p. 10.

13 January 1783. William HARRISON and Rebecca Underhill, dau. Mary Underhill. Sur. Giles Underhill. p. 32.

5 January 1789. William HARRISON and Mary Wilkerson. Sur. Nathan Wilkerson. Returned May 1789 by Rev. George Parham. p. 54.

16 August 1794. William HARRISON and Mary Gee. Sur. John Potts. p. 74.

5 December 1805. John HART and Martha C. Hall. Sur. Pleasant Hunnicutt. p. 119.

23 February 1803. Robert HART and Charity Hart. Married 24 February by Rev. Drewry Lane who says Cherry. Sur. Josiah Freeman. p. 110.

30 July 1806. Charles HARTLEY and Elizabeth Seldge. Married 6 August by Rev. James Rogers. Sur. Miles Sledge. p. 121.

2 April 1789. Thomas HARTLEY and Elizabeth Bell, dau. Sylvanus Bell. Married 16 April by Rev. John Meglamore. Sur. Balaam Freeman. p. 55.

3 March 1797. Mark W. HARWELL and Lucy Hunt, dau. Thomas Hunt, Jr. Sur. William Pettway. Wit: John Hunt. p. 86.

29 March 1790. Peter HARWELL and Betsey Hawthorne. Sur. Isham Hawthorne. Wit: John and Francis Hawthorne. p. 60.

1 February 1799. Richard HARWELL, Jr. and Nancy Hobbs. Married 9 February by Rev. Augustine Heath. Sur. John Hawthorne. Wit: Richard Johnson. p. 92.

31 December 1807. Daniel HARWOOD and Nancy Adams Married 6 January 1808 by Rev. James Rogers. Sur. James Maclamore. p. 127.

14 July 1796. John HARWOOD and Rebecca Champion, dau. Charles Champion. Sur. George Moseley. p. 82.

18 March 1773. Phillip HARWOOD and Selah Rochel, dau. John Rachel, deceased. Sur. William Mason. p. 17.

31 December 1807. Thomas HARWOOD and Sally Mason. Married 21 January 1808 by Rev. Robert Murrell, Sr. Sur. Lewis Reese. p. 127.

5 February 1789. George HATCH and Mary Shaw Thompson, ward of George Rives who is surety. Wit: Thomas E. Rives and John Peebles. p. 55.

3 March 1796. Thomas HATTON and Mary Jennett. Sur. John Lilly. Married 24 March by Rev. Henry Moss. p. 81.

24 December 1800. Henry HAWTHORN and Polly Moss, dau. Joshua Moss. Sur. Isaac Bendall. p. 99.

4 February 1790. John HAWTHORN and Mary Hobbs. Sur. Thomas Whitfield. p. 59.

21 July 1806. Archer HAY (or Hey) and Mary Sammons. Married by Rev. James Gibbons. Ministers' Returns p. 284.

27 December 1784. Benjamin HAY and Margaret Hay. Married by Rev. John Meglamore. Ministers' Returns. p. 323.

7 April 1808. Enos HAY and Polly Andrews, dau. Elizabeth Andrews. Married 14 April by Rev. Robert Murrell, Sr. of Southampton County. Sur. James Seaborne. p. 128.

18 December 1806. Gilbert HAY and Fanny Rollings, age 17. Married 2 January 1807 by Rev. James Rogers. Sur. Jesse Tudor. Wit: Sally Rollings. p. 122.

17 December 1785. John HAY and Martha Raley. Married by Rev. John Meglamore. Ministers' Returns p. 258.

8 January 1801. Richard HAY and Louisa Seaborne. Sur. Thomas Avent. p. 100.

30 November 1807. William HAY and Elizabeth Rollins, dau. Sally Rollins. Married 2 December by Rev. James Rogers. Sur. Curtis Lynn. p. 126.

17 November 1785. John HAYS and Martha O'Riley, dau. Thomas O'Riley, deceased. Sur. David Mason. p. 40.

5 December 1801. Benjamin HAYWOOD and Patsy Tuder, dau. Henry Tuder. Sur. Charles Holt. p. 103.

9 November 1793. Freeman HEARN and Mary Spain. Married 10 November by Rev. William Brown. Sur. William Hill Spain. p. 72.

1 December 1796. Edmund HEATH and Elizabeth Gibbons, dau. Lucy Gibbons. Sur. Robert Ray. Wit: Joshua Hawthorne. p. 84.

16 January 1794. Herbert HEATH and Mary Lee, dau. James Lee. Married 3 February by Rev. George Parham. Sur. Reaps. Mitchell. p. 73.

24 February 1781. Joseph HEATH, Jr. and Jane Gee, age 21, dau. Henry Gee. Sur. Joseph Heath, Sr. Wit: John H. Claiborne and Elizabeth Gee. p. 28.

20 December 1787. Nathan HEATH and Elizabeth Dunn. Sur. William Cureton. p. 49.

30 October 1780. Thomas HEATH and Selah Rives. Sur. Timothy Rives. p. 26.

16 March 1807. Thomas D. HEATH and Susanna Nicholson. Married 17 March by Rev. Drewry Lane. Sur. Benjamin B. Rosser. Wit: Jere Cobbs. p. 124.

6 October 1803. Tinsley HEATH and Ann Lloyd. Sur. Robert Brister. p. 112.

4 February 1808. Uriah C. HEATH and Betsey Howard. Married 10 February by Rev. James Rogers. Sur. John Moyler. p. 128.

11 January 1809. George HELVIN and Jane E. Wooten, ward of
Benjamin Cobb. Married 12 January by Rev. Drewry Lane who says
Jane C. Sur. William Norsworthy. p. 131.

21 December 1781. Stephen HERRING and Amey Parham, dau. Matthew
Parham. Stephen Herring of Lunenburg County. Sur. Thomas Mitchell.
Wit: John Mitchell. p. 29.

26 December 1780. William HERRING and Susannah Parham, dau.
Matthew Parham. William Herring of Lunenburg County. Sur. Peter
Raney. Wit: James Parham and Amey Parham. p. 27.

25 November 1783. Thomas HICKS and Rebecca White. Married by Rev.
John Meglamore. Ministers' Returns p. 322.

17 September 1785. John HIGHT and Nancy Glover. Married by Rev.
Jesse Lee. Ministers' Returns p. 259. See Thomas Hite.

20 May 1773. Green HILL and Mary Booth, dau. George Booth,
deceased. Sur. George Booth. p. 17.

1 July 1786. Herbert HILL and Charity Jarrad. Sur. Henry Jarrad,
Sr. Wit: Thomas Hunt. p. 42.

26 August 1794. John HILL and Sally Owen. Sur. Thomas Hill. p. 74.

16 September 1762. Michael HILL and Nancy Tyus. Sur. John Tyus.
p. 7.

Between 25 September 1771 and 10 October 1772. Allen HINES and
Frances Williams. Married by Rev. John Meglamore. Ministers'
Returns p. 257.

--------- 1791. Allen HINES and Judah Parker. Married by Rev.
John Meglamore. Ministers' Returns p. 265.

2 January 1788. Edwin HINES and Mary Cross. Sur. John Cross.
p. 49.

26 May 1802. George HINES and Elizabeth E. Chappell. Sur. William
Wright. p. 106.

15 March 1771. Hartwell HINES and Elizabeth Edmunds, widow.
Hartwell son of Joshua Hines who consents. Sur. Frederick Hines.
Wit: John Renn. p. 14.

21 August 1777. Howell HINES and Nancy Collier, dau. Sampson
Collier. Sur. Richard Parker. p. 22.

16 October 1797. Willie HINES and Nancy Hunt. Married 17 October
by Rev Drewry Lane. Sur. Benjamin Peete. p. 85.

7 October 1800. Chanal HITE and Rhody Hite. Sur. Simmons Hite.
Wit: John Hite. p. 98.

22 December 1781. Julius HITE and Agnes Land, dau. Robert Land.
Married 23 December by Rev. John Meglamore. Sur. John Hite.
Wit: George Goodwyn. p. 36.

15 December 1809. Robert HITE and Susanna Hobbs. Sur. James A.
Wren. Wit: William Parsons. p. 134.

30 November 1784. Thomas HITE and Elizabeth Land, dau. Robert
Land. Sur. Julius Hite. Wit: Richard Tomlinson. p. 35.

17 September 1785. Thomas HITE and Nancy Glover (Glovier), age
23, dau. Robert and Mary Glovier. Sur. John H. Claiborne. Wit:
Benjamin Baird. p. 39.   See John Hight.

19 November 1787. William HIX and Susanna Norris, dau. Joseph
Norris. Sur. Edward Fason. Wit: Beverly Booth. p. 48.

7 February 1794. Edmund HOBBS and Sally Pettway. Sur. William
Hobbs. p. 73.

15 January 1789. Isham HOBBS and Elizabeth Clarke, dau. Eve
Clarke. Sur. Thomas Hobbs. p. 54.

21 May 1778. Laburn HOBBS and Mary Whitfield. Sur. Thomas
Whitfield. p. 24.

12 February 1796. Peyton HOBBS and Elizabeth Tomlinson, consent
of Mary Tomlinson, Father lives out of Virginia. Sur. Miles
Tucker. p. 80.

16 March 1787. Stephen HOBBS and Amey Sturdivant. Married 17
March by Rev. John Meglamore who says Anney. Sur. James Glover,
Sr. Wit: Holum Sturdivant and James Eppes. p. 46.

19 October 1776. Thomas HOBBS and Rebecca Glover, dau. James
Glover who is surety. p. 21.

21 December 1789. William HOBBS and Martha (Patty) Whitfield,
consent of Thomas Whitfield. Married 24 December by Rev. Henry
Moss. Sur. William Whitfield. p. 58.

24 December 1754. Francis HOBSON and Frances Judkins, dau.
Charles Judkins. Sur. Thomas Dunn Jones. p. 1.

3 November 1809. Carter HOGWOOD and Lucy Adams. Married 8
November by Rev. James Rogers. Sur. Burwell Gilliam. p. 134.

28 July 1795. James HOGWOOD and Viney Richardson, dau. Elizabeth
Richardson. Sur. Charles Holt. p. 78.

2 June 1803. John HOGWOOD and Celia Adams. Sur. Barham Newsom.
p. 111.

9 November 1805. Ranson HOGWOOD and Amy Tudor, dau. Henry Tuder, Jr. Married 5 December by Rev. James Rogers. Sur. Benjamin Hogwood. p. 118.

5 November 1801. William HOGWOOD and Polly Adams. Sur. John Phipps. p. 103.

19 October 1796. Charles HOLDSWORTH and Elizabeth Cole. Married 22 October by Rev. Drewry Lane. Sur. Thomas Clary. Wit: Thomas Clary, Jr. and Sally Wright Cole. p. 84.

2 November 1808. John HOLDSWORTH and Polly Cornwell. Married 3 November by Rev. Drewry Lane. Sur. Jonathan Coker. Wit: Nancy D. White. p. 129.

1 October 1789. Robert White HOLDSWORTH and Mary Garland. Robert son of Charles Holdsworth. Sur. Richard Andrews. Wit: Samuel Summerell and B. Holdsworth. p. 56.

16 December 1799. David HOLLOWAY and Hannah Brown. Married 24 December by Rev. Drewry Lane. Sur. Lawrence Faison. p. 95.

30 July 1787. Herbert HOLLOWAY and Peggy Smith, dau. Lawrence Smith. Sur. James Holloway. p. 47.

4 November 1789. John Patrick HOLLOWAY and Nancy Kenibrugh. Married 9 November by Rev. Henry Moss. Sur. James Kennibrugh. p. 57.

20 October 1807. John HOLLOWAY and Rebecca Stacy. Married 24 October by Rev. Drewry Lane. Sur. Henry Harrison. p. 126.

16 December 1783. Thomas HOLLOWAY and Susanna Judkins. Sur. Thomas Ellis. Wit: Littleberry Mason. p. 32.

30 November 1801. Herbert HOLD and Betsy Holt. Sur. Charles Holt. p. 103.

5 September 1799. John HOLT and Fanny M. Harwood, dau. John Harwood. Sur. James Pennington. p. 94.

28 May 1804. John HOLT and Susanna Moore. Sur. Isaac Andrews. p. 115.

27 September 1781. Micajah HOLT and Sally Newsum, dau. of Thomas Newsum who is surety. Married 4 October by Rev. John Meglamore. p. 29.

10 June 1806. David HORN and Salley Loftin. Married 12 June by Rev. James Rogers. Sur. Jonathan Harrup. p. 121.

24 December 1805. Ephraim HORN and Eliza Booth. Married 26 December by Rev. James Rogers. Sur. Shadrack Horn. p. 119.

3 November 1796. Frederick HORN and Clarissa Hartley. Sur. Robert Horn. p. 84.

3 January 1797. Harmon HORN and Prudence Knight. Sur. Matthew Whitehead. Double wedding: see Matthew Whitehead. p. 85.

19 December 1805. Howell HORN and Patsey Wilborne. Married 25 December by Rev. James Rogers. Sur. Richard Horn. p. 119.

26 February 1805. James HORN and Judith Fogg. Married 27 February by Rev. James Rogers. Sur. Thomas Chambliss. p. 117.

28 October 1791. Richard HORN and Susannah Hill. Sur. John Hill. Married by Rev. William Brown. p. 64.

17 November 1795. Robert HORN and Rebecca Zills. Sur. Jesse Zills. Married by Rev. Henry Moss. p. 79.

3 September 1795. Shadrach HORN and Rebecca Hill. Sur. James Horn. p. 78.

23 January 1809. Crawley HOUSE and Nancy Stewart, dau. William Stewart. Married 26 January by Rev. James Rogers. Sur. Robert W. Land. Wit: William Johnson and Charles Stuart. p. 131.

21 December 1780. Henry HOWARD and Jane Jones, infant (under age), dau. James B. Jones. Henry Howard of Surry County. Sur. George Rives. Wit: Samuel Jones and John Jones. p. 27.

11 March 1771. Thomas HOWARD and Mary Baylis, infant (under age), dau. Humphrey Baylis. Thomas infant (under age), son of Henry Howard. Sur. John Watkins, Jr. Wit: Will Evans. p. 14.

9 January 1758. William HOWELL and Hannah Wyche, dau. George Wyche, deceased. Sur. Benjamin Wyche. p. 3.

19 May 1786. James HOWLE and Pamelia Tyus, dau. Benjamin Tyus. Married 20 May by Rev. John Cameron. Sur. Alexander Harrison. p. 42.

18 December 1792. Henry HUBBARD and Feraby Mosby, dau. Mrs. Martha Slate. Sur. William Clanton. Married 24 December by Rev. William Brown who says Pherabe Mosely. p. 70.

31 August 1801. James HUBBARD and Clary Linn. Sur. James Sammons. p. 102.

5 December 1785. Pleasant HUNNICUTT and Mary Cocke. Sur. Benjamin Mason. Married 8 December by Rev. John Cameron of Bristol Parish who says Mary Cooke. p. 40.

24 May 1802. Pleasant HUNNICUTT and Mary S. Harrison. Sur. John Chappell. p. 106.

15 March 1756. John HUNT and Elizabeth Mary Tyus, dau. John Tyus who is surety. p. 2.

20 May 1803. John HUNT and Rhoda Pettway, dau. John Pettway of North Carolina, deceased, and ward of Sterling Harwell of Halifax, North Carolina; resides with Mason Hartwell in Sussex County, Virginia. Sur. Christopher Rives. p. 111.

26 December 1798. Robert HUNT and Elizabeth Hargrave. Sur. Joseph Williamson. p. 92.

22 March 1765. Thomas HUNT and Dorothy Vaughan, dau. Thomas Vaughan who is surety. p. 9.

10 December 1786. Thomas HUNT and Amey Clements. Sur. Robert Bailey. Wit: William Chappell. p. 44.

9 April 1787. Balaam HUTCHINGS and Milley Barham. Married 17 April by Rev. John Meglamore. Sur. Henry Sosberry. Wit: Walter Gilliam. p. 47.

23 February 1782. Surrel (Burwell) HUTCHINS and Patty Felts. Married by Rev. John Meglamore. Ministers' Returns. p. 257.

13 August 1795. John HUTCHINGS and Edith Moss. Sur. Burwell Hutchings. p. 78.

21 June 1802. Peyton HUTCHINGS and Caty Hutchings, consent of Martha Hutchens. Sur. William Pelts. Wit: Buckner Lanier. Married by Rev. James Rogers. p. 107.

20 December 1784. James INMAN and Sarah Wallis. James Inman of Southampton County. Sur. Jesse Wallis. Married by Rev. John Meglamore. p. 36.

5 December 1791. James INMAN and Elizabeth White. Sur. Warren White. p. 65.

1 October 1796. James INMAN and Susannah Cross. Sur. William Cross. Married by Rev. Drewry Lane. p. 83.

16 December 1771. John IRBY and Rebecca Briggs, dau. George Briggs. Sur. Richard Blunt. Wit: Thomas Edmunds. p. 15.

5 August 1790. David IVEY and Susannah Pate, consent of Thomas Pate. Sur. John Pate. Wit: Peebles Ivey and Jesse Pate. Married by Rev. John Meglamore. p. 60.

4 June 1801. Eldridge IVEY and Eady Ivey, dau. Aaron Ivey. Sur. Henry Pate. p. 101.

30 March 1787. Jesse IVEY and Sarah Anderson. Married 7 April by Rev. Jesse Lee. Sur. James Eppes. p. 46.

15 December 1774. Joshua IVIE and Elizabeth Jarratt, dau. Henry. Jarratt (Jarrad). Sur. John Baird, Jr. Wit: Mary Jarrad and Sarah Jarrad. p. 19.

5 August 1790. David IVY and Susanna Pate. Married by Rev. John Meglamore. Ministers' Returns p. 265.

12 June 1771. Peter IVY and Mary Knight, age 21, dau. John and Elizabeth Knight. Sur. Timothy Rives. p. 14.

24 August 1779. Reuben JACKSON and Catey Woodrooff, dau. George Woodroof. Sur. Augustine Claiborne. Wit: Benjamin Woodroof and Patience Woodroof. p. 25.

6 December 1806. Robert JACKSON and Catharine Jackson, dau. Rheuten Jackson. Married 17 December by Rev. Augustine Heath. Sur. Frederick Jackson. p. 122.

5 December 1785. William JACKSON and Sally Eckles, dau. John Eckles. Married 15 December by Rev. John Cameron. Sur. Wood Heath. Wit: Frances Jackson. p. 40.

22 December 1810. Moland JAMES and Catharine Harris. Sur. John Birdsong. p. 138.

24 July 1781. Henry JARRAD and Peggy Bryan. Sur. Joshua Ivey. p. 28. See Henry Jarratt.

3 December 1805. Joseph JARRAD and Rebecca Ellis. Married 5 December by Rev. Drewry Lane. Sur. John Jarrad. p. 119.

2 December 1802. Nicholas JARRAD (Jarrett) and Polly Brown. Sur. John Brown. p. 108.

4 January 1804. Samuel JARRAD and Nancy Hines. Married 19 January by Rev. Drewry Lane. Sur. Willie Hines. p. 113.

24 April 1799. William JARRAD and Lucy Wallis. Sur. Jesse Wallis. p. 93.

24 July 1781. Henry JARRATT and Peggy Bryan. Sur. Joshua Ivey. p. 28. See Henry Jarrad.

7 August 1806. William JARRATT and Mary (Polly) Ivey, ward of Lewis Fort. Married 12 September by Rev. Robert Murrell, Sr. of Southampton County. Sur. John Jarratt. p. 121.

26 December 1793. Daniel JEFFERS and Elizabeth Moss. Married by Rev. Henry Moss. Ministers' Returns p. 268. See Daniel Jefferson.

5 December 1793. Daniel JEFFERSON and Elizabeth Moss. Sur. William Harrison. p. 72. See Daniel Jeffers.

25 February 1793. Burwell JENNINGS and Anne Rogers. Sur. Howell Underhill. p. 71.

6 March 1795. Burwell JENNINGS and Mary Plesent (Pleasants), age 24. Sur. William Scoggins. p. 76.

27 January 1798. Laban JENNINGS and Elizabeth Freeman, age over 18. Married 30 January by Rev. Drewry Lane. Sur. William Johnson. p. 88.

14 February 1803. Littleberry JENNINGS and Mary Bains, dau. Jesse Bains, Sr. Married 24 February by Rev. Drewry Lane who says Banns. Sur. Peter Jennings. p. 110.

18 February 1804. Peter JENNINGS and Creacy Bains, dau. Jesse Bains, Sr. Married 23 February by Rev. Drewry Lane. Sur. Littleberry Jennings. p. 113.

18 February 1788. Benjamin JOHNSON and Judah Chambliss, dau. William Chambliss. Sur. Theodorick Chambliss. p. 50.

7 November 1803. Benjamin JOHNSON and Frances Malone. Sur. Thomas Malone. p. 112.

21 December 1780. Collins JOHNSON and Sally Gilliam, dau. Levy Gilliam. Sur. Arthur Williamson. Wit: Henry Freeman and Levy Rotchel. p. 27.

6 October 1791. Edmund JOHNSON and Elizabeth Magee. Sur. John Magee. Married by Rev. William Brown. p. 64.

4 November 1789. Joel JOHNSON and Rebecca Sledge. Married 5 November by Rev. Henry Moss. Sur. Edward Fason. p. 57.

24 August 1786. Joshua JOHNSON and Elizabeth Jones. Sur. James Johnson. p. 43.

30 October 1806. Josiah JOHNSON and Nancy Bryant, dau. Jesse Bryant. Married 31 October by Rev. Drewry Lane. Sur. Benjamin O'Donniley. p. 121.

3 December 1768. Lewis JOHNSON and Mary Heron, dau. James and Mary Heron. Sur. William Mason. Wit: James Bell and William Ezell. p. 12

16 September 1772. Lewis JOHNSON and Lucy Ezell, dau. Isham Ezell. Sur. Cuthbert Stafford. Wit: John Lewis. p. 16.

20 February 1767. Moses JOHNSON and Agnes Battle. Sur. John Edmunds. Wit: Edward Fisher. p. 10.

5 March 1795. Moses JOHNSON and Elizabeth Groves Rose. Sur.
William Richardson. p. 76.

4 October 1802. Nicholas JOHNSON and Susanna Atkinson. Married 7
October by Rev. Drewry Lane. Sur. Jesse Bryant. Wit: Johnson
Atkinson. p. 107.

5 January 1792. Robert JOHNSON and Rebecca Betts. Married 12
January by Rev. Drewry Lane. Sur. Drewry Betts. p. 65.

5 February 1807. Robert JOHNSON and Nancy Hix. Married 12 February
by Rev. Drewry Lane. Sur. Henry Hix. Wit: James A. Wren. p. 124.

24 January 1796. Swan JOHNSON and Patsey Ezell. Sur. Charles
Spiers. Wit: Silvanus Bell. p. 80.

18 January 1788. Thomas JOHNSON and Sarah Hicks. Sur. John Hicks.
p. 49.

4 January 1779. William JOHNSON and Mary Dunn. William Johnson
of Amelia County. Sur. William Dunn, Sr. p. 24.

22 December 1801. William JOHNSON and Sally Smith. Sur. Joseph
Moore. p. 104.

3 July 1800. Benjamin Waddill JOHNSTON and Polly Bailey. Sur.
William Hall. Wit: Nathaniel Land. p. 97.

11 June 1807. Joel JOHNSTON and Sillar Johnson. Sur. Collins
Johnston. Married by Rev. James Rogers. p. 125.

12 October 1796. Camp JOINER and Elizabeth Rollings, dau. Susanna
Rollings. Sur. Charles Southward. Wit: Edwin Long. p. 83.

18 November 1801. Daniel JOLLY and Nancy Harrison. Sur. William
Harrison. p. 103.

30 December 1782. Abraham JONES and Martha Moss, consent of Henry
Moss. Sur. Edmund Moss. Wit: Robert Jones. p. 32.

27 July 1781. Binns JONES and Elizabeth Cargill, ward of Cyrill
Avery. Binns Jones of Brunswick County. Sur. John Cocke. p. 28.

21 August 1788. David JONES and Elizabeth Green. Sur. Drewry
Parker. Wit: Joshua Owen. p. 51.

7 December 1762. Edmund JONES and Rebecca Johnson, dau. William
Johnson. Edmund brother of James Jones. Sur. Henry Gee. Wit:
Hugh Belsher. p. 7.

7 June 1804. Edward JONES and Dolly Carter, dau. Harris Carter.
Sur. Williamson Smith. p. 115.

18 August 1774. Frederick JONES and Susanna Claiborne, dau. Col. Augustine Claiborne who is surety. p. 19.

19 December 1792. George JONES and Anna Parham. Married 20 December by Rev. Henry Moss. Sur. Gabriel Moss. p. 70.

4 July 1774. Hamilton JONES and Joceobina Willis. Sur. John Cargill. p. 19.

15 December 1783. Howell JONES and Elizabeth Booth. Sur. William Birdsong. Wit: Moses Booth, John Sikes and Richard Bailey. p. 34.

17 January 1788. Howell JONES and Polly Moore. Sur. Barham Moore. Married 14 February by Rev. John Meglamore. p. 49.

24 July 2809. Howell JONES and Lurana Gilliam. Sur. Hinchy Knight. p. 133.

14 October 1754. James Boiseau JONES and Ann Gilliam, dau. Hinchia Gilliam, deceased. Sur. David Jones. p. 1.

19 October 1765. James JONES and Rebecca Jones, widow of Edmund Jones, dau. of William Johnson. Edmund and James Jones were brothers. Sur. William Jones. Wit: Nicholas Massenburg. p. 9.

23 June 1774. Capt. James JONES and Leah Wyche, widow of James Wyche (nee Maclin). Sur. Augustine Claiborne. p. 19.

16 July 1757. Jesse JONES and Alce Stagg. Sur. Andrew Froughton. p. 3.

22 July 1758. John JONES and Elizabeth Binns, dau. Charles Binns, deceased, ward of Judith Hay. Sur. John Hay. p. 4.

20 September 1787. John JONES and Angelila Avent. Sur. Thomas Avent. p. 48.

19 March 1806. John JONES and Nancy Bowles. Married 20 March by Rev. James Rogers. Sur. Henry Bowles. p. 120.

12 February 1807. John JONES and Sacky Cypress. Married by Rev. Drewry Lane. Ministers' Returns p. 283.

18 August 1777. Mordecai JONES and Elizabeth Barnes, widow. Mordecai Jones of Brunswick County. Sur. John Cargill. p. 22.

24 January 1798. Richard JONES and Elizabeth Jones, dau. Robert Jones. Sur. Benjamin Peete. Married by Rev. Stith Parham. p. 88.

5 October 1789. Samuel JONES and Lilley Holloway. Sur. Lawrence Smith. p. 56.

6 November 1794. Samuel JONES and Salley Walter Butler, ward of Harris Carter. Sur. Richard Jones. p. 75.

18 December 1806. Wilie JONES and Willy Hargrave. Sur. John Jones. p. 122.

22 May 1767. William JONES and Elizabeth Hunt. Sur. John Peters. p. 11.

16 December 1797. Henry JORDAN and Susanna Barker. Married 21 December by Rev. Drewry Lane. Sur. Wyatt Ellis. p. 87.

11 February 1785. John JORDAN and Elizabeth Nicholson, widow. Sur. Isaac Ellis. Wit: William Nicholson, Sr. p. 36.

21 March 1796. John JOYNER and Priscilla Gilliam. Sur. Goodrich Howell. p. 81.

4 December 1797. James JUDKINS and Polly Anderton. Sur. Colston Wallis. Married 21 December by Rev. Drewry Lane who says Andriton. p. 87.

30 January 1806. Samuel W. JUDKINS and Elizabeth M. Jarrad. Sur. John Jarrad. Married by Rev. Drewry Lane. p. 120.

14 May 1798. William JUDKINS and Peggy Wallis. Married 24 May by Rev. Drewry Lane. Sur. Jesse Wallis. p. 90.

2 June 1767. John JUSTISS and Sarah Cook, dau. Reubin and Ann Cook. Sur. Benjamin Hill. Wit: Henry Cook. p. 11.

22 June 1784. Andrew KELSEY and Ruth Wilcox. Sur. John Bryar. p. 35.

17 November 1766. George KERR and Elizabeth Briggs. Sur. Augustine Claiborne. Wit: William Mason. p. 10.

7 August 1800. Andrew KERWIN (Carwin) and Elizabeth Rose. Sur. Thomas Fletcher. p. 97.

1 January 1788. John KEY and Nancy Loftin. Sur. Frederick Loftin. p. 49.

20 November 1788. Bingham KEYS and Susanna Eckels, dau. Mary Eckols. Married 27 November by Rev. Jesse Lee. Sur. Francis Jackson. p. 52.

2 April 1789. William KEYS and Elizabeth Griffin. Sur. Reuben Jackson. Returned May 1789 by Rev. George Parham. p. 55.

7 January 1796. Meredith KING and Lucy Davis. Sur. Baxter Davis. p. 80.

17 January 1805. Drewry KITCHEN and Fanny Davison. Sur. Henry Jordan. Married 16 February by Rev. Drewry Lane. p. 117.

21 February 1809. Enos KITCHEN and Polly J. Rainey, dau. Peter Rainey. Sur. Peter Booth. p. 132.

26 February 1787. Jesse KITCHEN and Sally Jones Hinton. Married 1 March by Rev. John Meglamore. Sur. Frederick Hines. Wit: Charles Hicks. p. 46.

6 December 1798. Ephraim KNIGHT and Patsy Sledge. Returned 12 January 1799 by Rev. Stith Parham. Sur. Robert Sturdivant. p. 92.

3 January 1793. James KNIGHT and Betsy Studivant. Married 17 January by Rev. William Brown. Sur. Matthew Sturdivant. p. 70.

3 November 1796. John KNIGHT and Charlotte Hood. Sur. Harmon Horn. p. 84.

21 October 1800. John KNIGHT and Lucy Jones, dau. Robert Jones. John Knight of Halifax, North Carolina. Sur. William Parham. Married by Rev. Stith Parham. p. 98.

28 July 1794. Moses KNIGHT, Jr. and Peggy Wynne. Sur. Robert Parham. p. 74.

24 December 1799. William KNIGHT and Nancy Whitfield. Married 28 December by Rev. Stith Parham. Sur. Ephraim Knight. p. 95.

28 September 1801. Robert LAINE and Susanna Raines. Married 1 October by Rev. Samuel Risher who says Lane. Sur. Peter Laine. p. 102. See Robert Lane.

3 February 1791. John Curtis LAMB and Nancy Barlor. Sur. John Lamb, Sr. p. 62.

10 May 1786. William LAMB and Agness Briggs. Sur. Daniel Lamb. Wit: Michael Bailey. p. 42.

27 June 1788. James LANCASTER and Rebecca Wallis (Wallace), dau. Jesse Wallace. Sur. Vines Turner. Wit: Betsy Turner. p. 51.

23 November 1786. Charles LAND and Mary Cooper. Married by Rev. John Meglamore. Ministers' Returns p. 260.

30 April 1792. Lewellen LAND and Mary Jones. Sur. William Land. p. 67.

16 December 1784. Nathaniel LAND and Sally Goodwyn. Married 23 December by Rev. John Meglamore. Sur. Jonathan Harris. p. 36.

14 April 1787. Robert LAND and Martha Chappell. Married 16 April by Rev. John Meglamore. Sur. Robert Bailey. p. 47.

4 February 1795. Robert LAND and Elizabeth Hawthorne. Sur. Benjamin B. Rosser. p. 76.

17 January 1798. Robert LAND and Sally Andrews. Sur. Henry
Andrews. p. 88.

23 October 1792. William LAND and Elizabeth Armstrong, dau. Robert
Armstrong. Sur. George Armstrong. p. 68.

25 November 1809. Drury LANE, Jr. and Susanna Andrews. Sur.
Jeremiah Lane. p. 134.

9 July 1807. John B. LANE and Nancy Clary, consent of Benjamin
Clary, Sr. and Nancy Clary. Sur. William Lane. Married by Rev.
Drewry Lane. p. 125.

8 March 1796. Peter LANE (Layne) and Jane Nicholson. Married 10
March by Rev. Drewry Lane. Sur. John Layne. Wit: Robert F.
Nicholson. p. 81.

1 October 1801. Robert LANE and Susanna Raines. Married by Rev.
Samuel Risher. Ministers' Returns p. 274. See Robert Laine.

6 December 1801. Abner LANIER and Sally Chambliss. Sur. Nathaniel
Chambliss. p. 137.

17 April 1783. Buckner LANIER and Rebecca Williamson, widow.
Sur. John McGlamore. p. 32.

25 September 1805. Edwin LANIER and Lucy Moss. Sur. Henry P.
Moss. Married by Rev. James Rogers. p. 118.

5 February 1788. Frederick LANIER and Rebecca Williamson, dau.
Jesse Williamson. Sur. Nathaniel Clanton. Wit: Henry and Temperance
Williamson. p. 50.

21 September 1778. Lewis LANIER and Anne Butler, dau. Thomas
Butler who is surety. Lewis son of Sampson Lanier. p. 24.

2 April 1759. Richard LANIER and Ann Mason, widow. Sur. William
Stuart. p. 5.

27 January 1785. William LASHLEY and Mary Robarts. Sur. Samuel
Jones. p. 36.

5 November 1789. William LAVENUT and Mary Figures, ward of Thomas
Edmunds. Sur. Robert Booth. Wit: M.M. Bailey. Returned February
1790 by Rev. George Parham. p. 57.

18 March 1800. James LEATH and Betsey Vinson. Sur. Joel Eckols.
p. 96.

20 October 1781. John LEATH and Lucretia Parham. Married by Rev.
Jesse Lee. Ministers' Returns p. 258.

17 December 1803. Richard LEATH and Polly Northcross. Sur. Robert Malone. p. 113.

6 December 1810. Jesse LEE and Nancy Weathers, dau. Mary Weathers. Sur. Jordan Edwards. p. 137.

15 February 1756. Peter LEE and Celia Pettway, dau. Robert Pettway. Peter son of Samuel Lee, who consents. Sur. Augustine Claiborne. p. 2.

20 December 1802. David LESSENBERRY and Sally Hobbs, dau. Rebecca Hobbs. Married 23 December by Rev. James Rogers. Sur. John T. Weathers. p. 109.

3 February 1769. John LESSENBERRY and Isabella Beddingfield, dau. Elizabeth Beddingfield. Sur. William Rives. p. 12.

6 February 1799. John LESSENBERRY and Patsy White. Married 14 February by Rev. Drewry Lane. Sur. James White. p. 92.

20 March 1807. William LESSENBERRY and Susan Harrison. Sur. William Harrison. Married by Rev. Joseph Hill. p.124.

12 November 1807. Edward LEWIS and Elizabeth Porch. Married by Rev. James Gibbons. Ministers' Returns p. 284.

13 March 1782. Enoch LEWIS and Lucy Barker, widow. Sur. Peter Jones. p. 30.

19 November 1787. Herbert LEWIS and Nancy Woodard, dau. Susana Woodard. Sur. Seth Tanner. p. 48.

4 December 1794. Jent LEWIS and Elizabeth Rowland. Sur. Charles Mitchell. p. 75.

1 October 1801. John LEWIS and Sixty Curtis. Sur. William Harper. p. 102.

3 November 1797. Joesph LEWIS and Selah Flowers. Sur. John Malone. Wit: Isaac Robinson. p. 87.

6 January 1798. Thomas LEWIS and Sally Avery, dau. Cyrill Avery. Sur. Nathaniel Peebles. p. 88.

6 February 1809. William LEWIS and Elizabeth Lee, dau. James Lee. Sur. Isham Cain, Jr. p. 131.

22 January 1782. ____LEYCESTER and Mary Dunn. Married by Rev. John Meglamore. Ministers' Returns p. 257.

31 May 1788. Frederick LILLY and Elizabeth Stokes. Sur. John Wynne. Married 11 June by Rev. John Melgamore. p. 51.

1 October 1789. John LILLY and Rebecca Jennett. Married 10 October by Rev. Henry Moss. Sur. Thomas Bailey. p. 56.

5 December 1803. John LILLY and Frances Smith. Married 15 December by Rev. James Rogers. Sur. Isaac Bendall. p. 113.

13 August 1799. Drewry LIVESAY and Frances Tucker. Sur. John Hall. Wit: Daniel Nives. p. 93.

2 February 1778. Charles LOCK and Martha Vaughan, dau. Thomas Vaughan. Charles Lock of Brunswick County. Sur. James Lock. p. 23.

19 December 1792. Henry LOFTIN and Keziah Champion, dau. Charles Champion. Sur. John Wall. p. 70.

7 February 1794. James LOFTIN and Silvia Bishop. Sur. Benjamin Bishop. p. 73.

26 July 1800. John LOFTIN and Nancy Smith, dau. Patience Smith. Sur. James C. Bailey. Married by Rev. Stith Parham. p. 97.

22 September 1802. Lewis LOFTIN and Susanna Moss, dau. Joshua Moss. Sur. Henry P. Moss. p. 107.

6 January 1790. Thomas LOFTIN and Martha Williamson. Married by Rev. John Meglamore. Ministers' Returns p. 263.

3 July 1794. Edwin LONG and Anna Andrews. Sur. Silas Long. Wit: Nancy Holt. p. 74.

27 February 1809. James LONG and Lucy Sills. Sur. William Clanton. Married by Rev. James Rogers. p. 132.

18 April 1810. John LONG and Angelila Freeman (Angelila Felts). Sur. William Clanton. p. 136.

14 December 1787. Lazarus LONG and Anne Williams, dau. James Williams. Sur. John Harwood. p. 49.

30 January 1788. Nicholas LONG and Rebecca Hill, dau. Margery Hill. Sur. Thomas Tyus. p. 50.

24 December 1788. Boland LONGBOTTOM and Rebecca Williams. Married by Rev. John Meglamore. Ministers' Returns p. 261. See Bolling Longbottom.

20 December 1788. Bolling LONGBOTTOM and Rebecca Williams. Sur. Philip Williams. Wit: William Milner. p. 53. See Boland Longbottom.

1 July 1786. Samuel LONGBOTTOM and Milley Seat. Sur. Josiah Seat. Wit: Thomas Hunt. Married 20 July by Rev. John Meglamore. p. 42.

17 December 1800. John LOVE and Betsy Welborne. Sur. William Fowler. Married by Rev. Stith Parham. p. 99.

19 March 1773. Charles LUCAS and Rebecca Jones, widow. Sur. Chappell Gee. p. 17.

30 November 1796. Stephen LUCAS and Rebecca B. Chappell. Sur. James Chappell. p. 84.

7 July 1803. John LYELL and Nancy S. Newsom, dau. Sally Newsom. Sur. John Jarratt. Wit: Robert Wrenn and Jare Adams. p. 111.

2 September 1790. Charles LYNN and Rebecca Davis. Married 5 September by Rev. John Mason. Sur. William Davis. p. 61.

14 November 1808. Curtis LYNN and Rebecca Long. Sur. James Long. p. 130.

15 November 1795. Abel MABRY and Mary Woodland. Sur. Isaac Adams. Returned 20 December by Rev. Stith Parham. p. 79.

12 January 1781. John MACKENNA and Rebekah Meachum, widow. Sur. Abdon Duff. p. 27.

6 November 1794. Burwell MACLIMORE and Mary Glover, dau. Jones Glover, Sr. Sur. Henry Loftin. p. 75.

21 December 1798. Edmund MACLIN and Elizabeth Pettway, niece of Mason and Mark Harwell. Sur. John Gibbons. p. 92.

1 January 1801. Benjamin MADLING and Nancy Barrw. Sur. Richard Madling. p. 100.

20 December 1787. Cary MAGEE and Ruth Land. Sur. John Magee. p. 49.

18 November 1786. David MAGEE and Judith Magee, consent of Priscilla Magee. Sur. David Mason. Married 23 November by Rev. John Meglamore. p. 44.

4 June 1789. David MAGEE and Mary Longbottom. Sur. Anselm Gilliam. p. 56.

9 November 1792. Drury MAGEE, Jr. and Mary Magee, dau. David Magee. Drury son of Drury Magee, Sr. Sur. James Davis. p. 69.

18 September 1788. Gilliam MAGEE and Elizabeth Gilliam. Sur. Anselm Gilliam. Married or returned 6 November by Rev. John Meglamore. p. 51.

27 December 1781. Harmon MAGEE and Patty Barham. Married by Rev. John Meglamore. Ministers' Returns p. 257.

22 January 1806. Henry MAGEE and Lucy Gilliam, dau. Elizabeth Gilliam. Henry son of William Magee. Married 24 January by Rev. James Rogers. Sur. George Booth. p. 120.

27 February 1794. John MAGEE and Temperance Knight. Sur. Gray Felts. Wit: Cary Magee and Edmund Johnson. Married by Rev. William Brown. p. 74.

15 July 1797. John MAGEE and Milly Rogers. Sur. Gilliam Magee. p. 85.

5 February 1802. Mial MAGEE and Sally Magee. Sur. John Bishop. p. 105.

6 February 1806. Mial (Michael) MAGEE and Nancy Cooper. Married 15 February by Rev. James Rogers. Sur. Howell Cooper. p. 120.

25 January 1803. William MAGET and Susanna Lonsford. Sur. Colston O. Wallis. Wit: John Holdsworth. p. 110.

19 January 1786. William MAGGOT and Molly Barker. Married 26 January by Rev. John Meglamore. Sur. Jesse Wallice. p. 41.

11 January 1808. William MAGEE and Lucy Magee, consent of Wiley Magee. Married 15 January by Rev. James Rogers. p. 127.

3 December 1807. Benjamin MALONE and Judith Q. Moyler. Married by Rev. James Rogers. Sur. Thomas R. Moyler. p. 126.

3 December 1807. George MALONE and Martha Chambliss. Married by Rev. James Rogers. Sur. Nathaniel Chambliss. p. 126.

5 April 1804. Harper MALONE and Elizabeth Andrews. Married 19 April by Rev. Drewry Lane. Sur. John Andrews. p. 114.

6 December 1804. John MALONE and Nancy Jordan. Married 20 December by Rev. Drewry Lane. Sur. Jesse Warren. p. 116.

12 December 1786. Nathaniel MALONE and Rebecca Winfield. Married 14 December by Rev. John Melgamore. Sur. Henry Winfield. Wit: William Vines and Mary Vines. p. 44.

7 December 1797. Thomas MALONE and Mary Chappell, dau. Thomas Chappell. Sur. William P. Walker. Wit: William and Thomas Malone. Married 16 December by Rev. Stith Parham. p. 87.

12 December 1798. Thomas MALONE and Rebecca Green, ward of Robert Buster. Married 13 December by Rev. Stith Parham. Sur. Thomas Cain. p. 92.

6 February 1800. Thomas MALONE and Polly Mason, dau. Thomas Mason. Married 13 February by Rev. Stith Parham. Sur. William Malone. Wit: Nathaniel Land and John Malone. p. 96.

1 October 1795. William MALONE and Mary Mangum. Sur. Samuel
Mangum. Married by Rev. George Parham. p. 78.

_____ 1801. William MALONE and Jane Wilborn. Married by Rev.
Stith Parham. Ministers' Returns p. 277.

13 November 1798. Balaam MANGUM and Winney Atkinson, consent of
Joel Atkison. Consent of Samuel Mangum as to Balaam. Sur. Thomas
Atkison. p. 91.

15 November 1779. Samuel MANGUM and Rebecca Cotton, dau. Richard
Cotton who is surety. p. 25.

18 November 1805. Christopher MANLOVE and Lucy Wright Carter,
dau. Harris Carter. Sur. Samuel Jones. p. 118.

13 February 1787. Peter MANRY and Martha Cornet, dau. Martha
Cornet. Married 15 February by Rev. John Meglamore. Sur. Henry
Hogwood. Wit: Jones Cornet. p. 46.

15 July 1800. Benjamin MARABLE and Lucy Hawthorn. Sur. Alfred
Moss. p. 97.

28 May 1806. Benjamin MARABLE and Patsey Pennington. Married 29
May by Rev. James Rogers. Sur. Henry P. Moss. p. 121.

29 October 1794. Edward MARABLE and Sally Penington, dau. Marcus
Penington. Sur. James Williamson. p. 75.

31 October 1775. Henry Hartwell MARABLE and Elizabeth Mason, dau.
Isaac Mason, deceased, and sister of John Mason. Sur. Hartwell
Marable, Sr. Wit: Lemuel Jones. p. 21.

16 December 1790. Matthew MARRABLE and Memima Mangum. Married
18 December by Rev. Henry Moss. Sur. James Glover, Jr. p. 62.

24 February 1782. Edward MARKS and Elizabeth Bishop. Married by
Rev. John Meglamore. Ministers' Returns p. 257.

6 December 1792. John MARKS and Nancy Ezell. Sur. Robert Andrews.
P. 69.

14 August 1804. Nathan MARKS and Sarah Bradley. Married 19
August by Rev. James Rogers. Sur. John Collier. p. 115.

29 December 1807. Anthony MASON and Patsey Lanier. Sur. Benjamin
B. Rosser. Married by Rev. James Rogers. p. 127.

10 April 1810. Charles J. MASON and Mary P. Adams. Sur. David
Grizzard. p. 136.

5 October 1809. Frederick MASON and Aney Avent. Married 18 October by Rev. Robert Murrell, Sr. of Southampton County. Sur. James Seaborne. p. 134.

16 October 1777. James MASON and Rebecca Thweat. Sur. Richard Parker. p. 23.

9 June 1760. John MASON, Jr. and Elizabeth Gee. Sur. John Mason and Henry Gee. p. 5.

17 March 1775. John MASON and Elizabeth Peters, dau. Thomas Peters. Sur. William Parker. Wit: Matthew Peters and John King. p. 20.

6 December 1804. John MASON, Jr. and Mary M. Neves, dau. Daniel Neves. John son of William Mason, deceased. Sur. John Winfield. p. 116.

5 October 1782. Peyton MASON and Polly Peebles, dau. Mary Peebles. Sur. John Mason. Wit: B. Claiborne and John Claiborne. p. 31.

21 September 1773. Richard MASON and Mary Burrow, widow. Sur. Nathaniel Newsome. p. 17.

16 January 1777. Thomas MASON and Lucy Jones, dau. Capt. James Jones. Sur. Flood Nicholson. Wit: George Booth and David Mason. p. 22.

7 June 1771. William MASON and Mary Gilliam, dau. William Gilliam, deceased, and Mary Gilliam. Sur. John Rives. Wit: John Sturdivent. p. 15.

25 July 1774. William MASON and Lucrecia Mason, dau. Major John Mason. Sur. Augustine Claiborne. p. 19.

24 July 1779. John MASSENBURG and Elizabeth Eldridge, dau. of William Eldridge, deceased, and Mrs. Ann Cargill who writes consent. Sur. Binns Jones. Wit: James Gee. p. 25.

18 September 1788. Avent MASSEY and Ann (Nancy) Owen. Sur. William Owen. Wit: William Grizzard. p. 52.

27 May 1807. William MASSEY and Nancy Grizzard. Married 28 May by Rev. James Rogers. Sur. Ambrose Grizzard. p. 125.

5 December 1782. Joseph MATTOX and Sarah Adkins, widow. Sur. James Grantham. p. 31.

17 December 1804. Isaac MEDLEN and Sarah Fiers, dau. John Fiers. Sur. Thomas Rowland. Wit: Thomas Chappell and Robert Chappell. p. 116.

7 June 1798. John MEGLAMORE and Polly Stuart. Sur. Charles Stuart. p. 90.

21 December 1781. John MEREDITH and Elizabeth Pennington. John Meredith of Dinwiddie County. Sur. Frederick Pennington. p. 29.

26 May 1763. Abraham MITCHELL, Jr. and Elizabeth Hines, dau. William Hines. Sur. Edmunds Jones. Wit: William Hines, Jr. p. 8.

5 June 1779. John MITCHELL and Scota Stewart, dau. William Stewart. Sur. Augustine Claiborne. Wit: John Stewart and William Cocke. p. 24.

13 September 1802. Luke MITCHELL and Luraney Harvill. Sur. Thomas Mitchell. p. 107.

5 February 1807. Paul MITCHELL and Nancy Seward. Married 12 February by Rev. Nathaniel Berriman, Sr. of Surry County. Sur. William Rives. Wit: Jones Mitchell and Benjamin Turner. p. 124.

29 December 1783. Reaps MITCHELL and Susanna Rives, dau. William Rives. Sur. McDuell Anderson. Wit: Robert Mitchell, James Rives and John Cook. p. 34.

27 February 1785. Thomas MITCHELL and Rebecca Stewart, dau. William Stewart. Sur. Joel Redding. Wit: John Stewart and Henry Hood. p. 37.

31 December 1792. Benjamin MONTGOMERY and Sarah Cook. Sur. Richard Cook. p. 70.

28 January 1794. Benjamin MOODY and Lilley Meachum, dau. Banks Meachum. Married 31 January by Rev. Henry Moss. Sur. Thomas Tarpley. p. 73.

5 February 1795. James MOODY and Priscilla Bullock. Sur. William Land. p. 76.

4 October 1802. Banister MOORE and Lucy Hutchings. Married 6 October by Rev. Drewry Lane. Sur. Banister Batts. p. 107.

31 December 1794. Charles MOORE and Nancy Holt, dau. Nathaniel Holt. Sur. David Wrenn. p. 75.

3 October 1793. James MOORE and Amey Wyche Holt. Sur. Charles Moore. Married by Rev. William Brown. p. 72.

20 May 1762. John MOORE and Mary Smith, dau. Edward Smith. Sur. William Hamlin. p. 6.

2 November 1789. John MOORE and Mildred Lucas Bell, dau. Mildred Bell. Married 3 November by Rev. John Meglamore. Sur. Silvanus Bell. Wit: Robert Pettway. p. 57.

11 October 1801. Joseph MOORE and Nancy Briggs. Married 22 October by Rev. Drewry Lane. Sur. Joseph Rosser. p. 103.

1 March 1790. Robert MOORE and Priscilla Jones. Sur. James Moore. p. 59.

19 December 1801. Tango MOORE and Lidda Chappell. Sur. Lewis Turner. p. 104.

18 October 1766. William MOORE and Elizabeth Flowers. Sur. James Jones. p. 10.

8 January 1798. John MORGAN and Sally Moseley. Sur. Henry Tuder. p. 88.

31 December 1774. William MORING and Lucy Massenburg, widow of Nicholas Massenburg. Sur. James Glover, Jr. p. 20.

13 June 1777. William MORING (Moreing) and Ann Barber Jones, dau. Lain Jones, deceased, consent of William Claiborne. Sur. Frederick Leigh. Wit: Sarah Wallis and Richard Lanier. p. 22.

13 December 1794. John MORRIS and Nancy Wootten. Married 18 December by Rev. Drewry Lane. Sur. Edward Wootten, Jr. p. 75.

24 November 1798. Nicholas MORRIS and Charlotte Cooper. Married 27 November by Rev. Drewry Lane. Sur. James Cooper. p. 91.

5 November 1795. Frederick MOSELEY and Rebecca Underwood, consent of Robert Wren. Sur. Isaac Bendall. p. 79.

7 July 1803. Hartwell MOSELEY and Rhoda Robertson. Sur. Hix Robinson. p. 111.

7 November 1791. William MOSELEY and Sally Tuder. Sur. Henry Tuder. Married by Rev. William Brown. p. 64.

5 December 1791. Alfred MOSS and Susanna Hawthorn. Married 10 December by Rev. Henry Moss. Sur. Thomas Bailey, Jr. p. 65.

22 August 1782. Edmund MOSS and Edith Barnett Gilbert. Sur. Hartwell Marable. p. 30.

19 December 1801. Edmund MOSS and Sally Whitfield. Sur. Ephraim Knight. p. 104.

25 April 1796. Gabriel MOSS and Elizabeth Oliver. Sur. William Fowler. Married by Rev. Stith Parham. p. 82.

22 July 1785. Henry MOSS and Keziah Freeman. Married 28 July by Rev. John Cameron of Bristol Parish. Sur. David Mason. p. 38.

4 January 1809. Henry MOSS and Abba Browne, dau. William Browne. Sur. Hinchey Knight. p. 131.

10 March 1810. Henry P. MOSS and Polly Wrenn. Sur. Benjamin Marable. p. 135.

15 June 1769. Joshua MOSS and Sarah Pennington, dau. John Pennington. Sur. Waddill Johnson. p. 13.

16 February 1786. William MOSS and Lydia Bishop. Sur. Nathan Bishop. Wit: Dixon Hall. Married 25 February by Rev. John Meglamore. p. 41.

4 December 1806. Thomas K. MOYLER and Susan Parham, consent of William Parham. Married 17 December by Rev. James Rogers. Sur. John Moyler. p. 122.

24 June 1805. Warren MURFREY and Jincy Clary. Married 4 July by Rev. Jesse Halleman, Sr. Sur. William Clary. p. 118.

21 August 1805. Jenkins MURPHEY and Polley B. Andrews. Married 29 August by Rev. Jesse Halleman, Sr. Sur. Charles Barker. p. 118.

18 March 1800. Charles MURPHREY and Lucy Judkins. Sur. Lemuel Bailey. Wit: James Judkins. p. 96.

30 March 1795. William MURPHY and Sarah Montgomery. Sur. Nathaniel Peebles. p. 76.

4 December 1784. Robert Murrell and Mary White. Robert Murrell of Dindiddie County. Sur. Thomas Peterson. p. 35.

9 February 1785. Howell MYRICK and Hannah Evans, dau. Benjamin Evans. Howell Myrick of Southampton County. Sur. Howell Jones. p. 36.

16 February 1782. James McCORMACK and Susanna Haile. Married by Rev. John Meglamore. Ministers' Returns p. 257.

22 January 1784. Dunkin McINLEY and Jiny Land. Married by Rev. John Meglamore. Ministers' Returns p. 323.

4 April 1799. Laithlim McKENNON and Martha Hewitt. Married 17 April by Rev. Stith Parham who says Lathlin. Sur. Robert Powell. p. 93.

9 November 1809. Gilliam McLEMORE and Jesey Wasdon. Married by Rev. Robert Murrell, Sr. of Southampton County. Ministers' Returns p. 275.

2 November 1809. Gilliam McLEMORE and Jincy Wasdin(?). Sur. William Pleasants. p. 134.

23 February 1786. Howell McLEMORE and Lucy Harris, dau. Lewis Harris. Sur. Samuel Jarrad. p. 42.

4 August 1796. James McLEMORE and Rebecca Harwood, dau. Daniel Harwood. Sur. Benjamin Adams. p. 82.

12 January 1782. Duncan McINDLEY and Rebecca Sammons. Married by Rev. John Meglamore. (McKinley?) Ministers' Returns p. 257.

27 December 1796. Thomas NANCE and Sally Heath, dau. Wood Heath. Sur. Joseph Cook. Wit: Henry Heath. p. 85.

24 August 1757. John NASH, Jr. and Elizabeth Fisher, dau. Charles Fisher, deceased. Wit: Mary Fisher. John Nash of Prince Edward County. Sur. Augustine Claiborne. p. 3.

4 October 1804. James NEBLETT and Frances Sturdivant. Married 12 October by Rev. James Rogers. Sur. Wilkins Whitfield. p. 116.

30 January 1805. Bolling NEW and Ann H. Stone. Sur. John Cross. p. 117.

3 November 1808. Bolling NEW and Mary Dunn. Sur. William Parham. Married 10 November by Rev. James Rogers who says Polly. p. 129.

30 January 1806. John NEWBY and Sally P. Jarrad. Sur. William Jarrad. Married by Rev. Drewry Lane. p. 120.

18 August 1780. Andrew NEWSOM and Elizabeth Fort. (Newsum) Sur. William Newsum. Wit: William Massenburg. p. 26.

19 January 1804. David NEWSOM and Patty Whitehorn, dau. John Whitehorn. Sur. John Jarratt. p. 113.

12 January 1797. Eldridge NEWSOM and Polly Harwood, dau. John A. Harwood. Sur. George Moseley. p. 85.

13 January 1786. Jacob NEWSOM and Polly Barham. Married by Rev. John Meglamore. Ministers' Returns p. 258.

21 December 1807. Nathaniel NEWSOM and Elizabeth Whitehorn. Sur. William Whitehorn. Married 22 December by Rev. James Rogers. p. 126.

6 October 1777. Thomas NEWSOM and Mary Jarratt, dau. Nicholas Jarratt who is surety. p. 23.

25 September 1810. Bryant NEWSOME and Polly Grizzard. Married 27 September by Rev. Robert Murrell of Southampton County. Sur. David Grizzard. p. 136.

20 October 1789. Charles NEWSUM and Temperance Holt, dau. Charles Holt. Married 29 October by Rev. John Meglamore. Sur. Thomas Peete. Wit: Patsey Holt. p. 56.

16 August 1785. Randall NEWSUM and Polly Isel. Married by Rev. John Meglamore. Ministers' Returns p. 258.

25 February 1758. Thomas NEWSUM and Alice Stagg, own consent. Sur. Andrew Troughton. p. 3.

6 January 1807. William H. NIBLETT and Lucresy Wynne, ward of John Wynne. Married 7 January by Rev. James Rogers. Sur. Ephraim Wynn. Wit: William Wynn. p. 123.

16 January 1777. Flood NICHOLSON and Mary Land, dau. of Robert Land. Flood Nicholson formerly from North Carolina. Sur. Thomas Mason. Wit: Mary Battle and Elizabeth Battle. p. 22.

16 November 1769. Harris NICHOLSON and Susanna Briggs, dau. George Briggs. Sur. Jesse Hargrave. Wit: Howell Briggs. p. 13.

16 April 1795. Harris NICHOLSON and Amelia Grg. Sur. Cadwallader Jones. p. 77.

10 April 1771. James NICHOLSON, Jr. and Elizabeth Woodroof, dau. Richard Woodroof of Brunswick County who is surety. Wit: John Baird. James Nicholson, Jr. age 21, of North Carolina, son of James and Anne Nicolson. p. 14.

7 May 1763. John NICHOLSON and Elizabeth Andrews, dau. John Andrews who is surety. p. 8.

5 May 1762. Michael NICHOLSON and Mildred Cheesman (Chisman), dau. George Cheesman, deceased. Michael, age 22, son of Robert Nicholson. Sur. Thomas Young. Letter from John Lamb certifies that Mildred is of age. p. 6.

6 September 1799. Robert NICHOLSON and Elizabeth Smith, dau. Patience Smith. Married 20 September by Rev. Stith Parham. Sur. Robert Smith. p. 94.

7 March 1796. Thomas NICHOLSON and Lucy Kitchen, consent of Benjamin Kitchen. Married 24 March by Rev. Drewry Lane. Sur. William Kitchen. Wit: Drury Kitchen. p. 81.

4 January 1790. Enoch NORRIS and Mary Hicks. Sur. William Hicks. Wit: Luke Norris. p. 58.

19 January 1793. Frederick NORTHCROSS and Sally Wilks Bell, consent of Mildred Bell. Married 22 January by Rev. William Brown. Sur. Peter Rainey. p. 70.

28 December 1809. George NORSWORTHY and Elizabeth Birt. Sur. Herod Birt. p. 135.

15 August 1808. John NORSWORTHY, Jr. and Patience Carrell. Sur. James Watkins. p. 129.

24 October 1801. James NORTHCROSS and Mary Malone. Sur. Frederick Northcross. p. 103.

1 May 1780. Nathan NORTHINGTON and Ann Stewart, dau. Richard Stewart. Sur. William Mason. Wit: John Mason and Nathaniel Mason. p. 26.

1 November 1798. Nathan NORTHINGTON and Jane Oliver. Married by Rev. Stith Parham. Sur. Theoderick Chambliss. p. 91.

3 December 1774. Samuel NORTHINGTON and Priscilla Mitchell, widow. Sur. William Dunn. p. 19.

1 July 1794. George NORWOOD and Winifred Rives. Married by Rev. William Brown. Ministers' Returns p. 269.

21 December 1807. Joel NUNNALLY and Sally Bishop. Married by Rev. James Gibbons. Ministers' Returns p. 284.

25 August 1781. James OBIRE and Elizabeth Leath. Married by Rev. Jesse Lee. Ministers' Returns p. 258.

5 February 1787. Augustine OGBURN and Elizabeth Massenburg. Sur. Michael Bailey. p. 46.

5 February 1787. Nicholas OGBURN and Mary Harrison. Sur. Richard Cooke. p. 46.

7 February 1799. Asia OLIVER and Fanny Myrick. Sur. William Hall. p. 93.

6 June 1799. Isaac OLIVER and Lucy Myrick. Sur. Jesse Wrenn. p. 93.

11 December 1789. Balaam OWEN and Sarah King, dau. Joshua King. Married 24 December by Rev. John Meglamore. Sur. William Owen. Wit: Edmund and Benjamin Owen. p. 58.

3 September 1795. David OWEN and Nancy Jarratt. Sur. John Jarratt. p. 78.

2 April 1807. David OWEN and Polly Bell. Married 16 April by Rev. James Rogers. Sur. James B. Jarratt. p. 124.

4 March 1800. Drury OWEN and Polly Wilborne. Married 5 March by Rev. Stith Parham. Sur. James Wilborne. p. 96.

18 May 1810. Ephraim OWEN and Ann Baird. Sur. Henry Dowden. p. 136.

5 May 1808. Jesse OWEN and Rebecca Malone. Married 25 May by Rev. James Rogers. Sur. Thomas Malone, Jr. p. 128.

11 October 1805. John OWEN and Betsy Smith, daughter-in-law (step-dau.) of Nicholas Presson. Married 16 October by Rev. Jesse Halleman, Sr. Sur. Lemuel Bain. p. 118.

6 October 1808. John C. OWEN and Zilla Lancaster, dau. James Lancaster, deceased. Ward of William Judkins. Married 13 October by Rev. James Rogers. Sur. Richard Sledge. p. 129.

1 October 1781. Joshua OWEN and Mary Chambliss, dau. William Chambliss, Sr. Married 4 October by Rev. John Melgamore. Sur. Benjamin Green. Wit: James Green. p. 29.

20 January 1784. Joshua OWEN and Sarah Green. Married by Rev. John Meglamore. Ministers' Returns p. 323.

5 July 1792. Nathan OWEN and Mary Griffin. Sur. John Bonner, Jr. Married by Rev. George Parham. p. 67.

29 June 1764. Robert OWEN and Lucy Stokes, age 22, dau. Sylvanus and Cecilia Stokes. Sur. John Berryman. p. 8.

21 October 1794. Robert OWEN and Charlotte Rives. Robert ward of Edmund Owen who is surety. p. 75.

15 April 1809. Samuel OWEN and Ann Chappell, dau. Thomas Chappell. Sur. Thomas Malone, Jr. Wit: John Raney and Lewis Owen. p. 132.

14 November 1800. William OWEN and Polly Lewis, consent of Manuel and Sally Lues (Lewis). Sur. Peter Cain. p. 98.

9 November 1781. James PAIR and Rebecca Bottom. Married by Rev. John Meglamore. Ministers' Returns p. 257.

4 November 1791. Marcus PAIR and Celia Booth. Married 29 November by Rev. Henry Moss. Sur. John Wynne. p. 64.

25 June 1798. Francis PALMER and Nancy King. Sur. John Hall. Married by Rev. Augustine Heath. p. 90.

25 December 1785. Anderson PARHAM and Nancy Parham. Married by Rev. Jesse Lee. Ministers' Returns p. 259.

27 January 1794. Booth PARHAM and Susanna Kelly Parham, dau. William Parham, Sr. Married 30 January by Rev. William Brown. p. 73.

13 November 1788. Cesar PARHAM and Judah Scott. Married by Rev. Jesse Lee. Ministers' Returns p. 261.

15 November 1764. Ephraim PARHAM and Hannah Hill. Sur. Richard Hill. p. 8.

19 March 1767. Ephraim PARHAM and Ruth Dunn, dau. Thomas Dunn who is surety. p. 10.

10 October 1796. Ephraim PARHAM and Jane Dunn. Married 12 October by Rev. Henry Moss. Sur. William Pettway. p. 83.

18 March 1785. James PARHAM and Molly Parham, dau. Nathaniel Parham. Sur. John Graves. Wit: Rebecca Winfield. p. 37.

27 September 1788. John PARHAM and Ann Winfield. Sur. Thomas Hartley. Wit: Seth and Lucretia Pool. p. 52.

27 August 1804. John PARHAM and Anne Jones, dau. Robert Jones. Married 30 August by Rev. James Rogers. Sur. Robert Jones, Jr. p. 115.

2 November 1809. John PARHAM and Barbara Massenburg. Married 9 November by Rev. James Rogers. Sur. John Massenburg. p. 134.

21 December 1806. Leonard H. PARHAM and Nancy Burk. Married 23 December by Rev. James Rogers. Sur. Jesse Owen. p. 123.

21 November 1792. Lewis PARHAM and Elizabeth Chappell. Sur. James Chappell. p. 69.

2 August 1802. Lewis PARHAM and Polly Gibbons, dau. Lucy Gibbons. Married 3 August by Rev. Stith Parham. Sur. Edward Pennington. p. 107.

9 October 1758. Nathaniel PARHAM and Celia Lee, widow of Peter Lee. Sur. Robert Pettway. p. 4.

19 January 1778. Robert PARHAM and Rebecca Berriman, infant (under age) dau. John Berriman. Robert son of Nathaniel Parham. Sur. John Massenburg. p. 23.

5 January 1792. Robert PARHAM and Hannah Eckles, dau. Mary Eckles. Sur. Francis Jackson. p. 65.

25 June 1804. Simon PARHAM and Polly Evans. Sur. Thomas Nance. p. 115.   See Simore Parham.

25 June 1804. Simore PARHAM and Polly Evans. Married by Rev. Augustine Heath. Ministers' Returns p. 280.   See Simon Parham.

2 September 1772. Stith PARHAM and Lucretia Parham, widow. Sur. Robert Tucker. Wit: Samuel Todd. p. 16.   Double wedding: See Robert Tucker.

3 December 1789. Thomas PARHAM and Rebecca Parham. Sur. John Malone. p. 58.

18 October 1799. Thomas PARHAM and Elizabeth Moody. Sur. William Parham. p. 94.

4 February 1802. Thomas PARHAM and Elizabeth Hall. Sur. William Wynne. Wit: Daniel Nives. p. 105.

18 September 1755. William PARHAM and Mary Stevens, dau. Edward Stevens, deceased. Sur. John Mason. p. 1.

7 October 1772. William PARHAM and Mary Kelly, dau. John Kelly. Sur. John Parham. Wit: Ann Foster and George Parham. p. 16.

18 December 1787. William PARHAM and Mary Comar. Married 21 December by Rev. Jesse Lee. Sur. Robert Bailey. p. 49.

6 December 1790. William PARHAM and Margaret Spain. Married 23 December by Rev. Jesse Lee. Sur. William Malone. p. 61.

4 December 1806. William PARHAM and Lucy Cross, dau. John Cross. Married 18 December by Rev. Drewry Lane. Sur. John Potts. p. 122.

15 June 1769. Drewry PARKER and Mildred Clanton, age 26, dau. Mary Clanton. Sur. Reuben Clanton. Wit: William Loftin. p. 13.

21 October 1791. Frederick PARKER and Temperance Williamson, consent of Jesse Williamson. Sur. Nathan Clanton. Married by Rev. William Brown. p. 64.

9 February 1760. Thomas PARKER and Sarah Parker, dau. William Parker. Sur. David Jones. p. 5.

17 March 1768. William PARKER and Mary Peters, infant (under age), dau. Thomas Peters, Sr. Sur. William Hines. Wit: James Peters. p. 11.

27 December 1771. William PARKER and Susanna Hunt, infant (under age), dau. Benjamin Hunt, deceased, and ward of William Hines. Sur. James Peters. Wit: John Peters. p. 15.

14 June 1805. Richard PARR and Lucy Davison. Married 20 June by Rev. Jesse Halleman, Sr. Sur. Herbert Sledge. Wit: Polly Epps. p. 117.

4 February 1793. Henry PARSONS and Hannah Stacy. Sur. Edmund Stacy. p. 70.

29 March 1804. Josiah PARSONS and Patsy Gee. Returned 3 May by Rev. Joesph Hill. Sur. William Parsons. Wit: Polly Harrison. p. 114.

24 December 1795. Robert PARSONS and Catharine Stacy. Married by Rev. Drewry Lane. Ministers' Returns p. 270. See Robert Parsons.

6 February 1806. William PARSONS and Susanna Loftin. Sur. Henry P. Moss. Married by Rev. James Rogers. p. 120.

30 July 1803. Littleberry PARTRIDGE and Frances Gilliam. Sur. Willis Partridge. p. 112.

4 November 1802. Cordy PATE and Catharine Hearne. Returned 2 December by Rev. Stith Parham. Sur. Henry Pate. p. 108.

22 April 1801. Hardy PATE and Polly Fisher, dau. Edward Fisher. Sur. John Pate. p. 101.

7 October 1802. Henry PATE and Elizabeth King. Sur. Cordy Pate. Married 2 November by Rev. Stith Parham. p. 108.

30 December 1800. Jesse PATE and Nancy Loftin. Sur. Tandolph Felts. p. 99.

10 December 1790. John PATE and Salley Prince, dau. John Prince. Sur. Allen Warwick. p. 61.

7 March 1793. John PATE and Sally Jones. Sur. William Pate. p. 71.

12 May 1804. John PATE and Rebecca Pate. Sur. Kinchen Felts. p. 115.

18 September 1777. Michael PAYNE and Ruana Fagan, widow. Sur. John Judkins. p. 23.

16 February 1786. Edmund PEEBLES and Harriett Harrison. Sur. James Walker. Wit: Nathaniel Jones. p. 41.

8 July 1785. Jesse PEEBLES and Scota Mitchell, widow of John Mitchell, dau. of William Stewart. Sur. William Chambliss. p. 38.

31 October 1785. Jesse PEEBLES and Elizabeth Sledge, dau. Amos Sledge, deceased, ward of James Epps. Married 1 November by Rev. Jesse Lee. Sur. William Chambliss, Jr. Wit: Timothy Rives. p. 39.

19 May 1763. Thomas PEEBLES and Mary Hancock, widow, dau. John Harrison who is surety. p. 8.

25 March 1785. Thomas PEEBLES and Mary Rives, age 21, dau. William Rives, deceased. Sur. William Sykes. Wit: Joel Rives. p. 37.

29 December 1790. William PEEBLES and Sarah Jarrat, consent of John Jarratt. Sur. Fortunatus Jarrat. p. 62.

21 December 1807. Edward PEGRAM and Dorothea Gilliam, dau. Martha Gilliam. Sur. William J. Hunt. Married by Rev. James Rogers. p. 127.

17 September 1793. Edward PENNINGTON and Elizabeth Pennington. Sur. Jesse Wrenn. p. 72.

13 December 1799. Edward PENNINGTON and Sally Judkins. Married 17 December by Rev. Stith Parham. Sur. William Johnston. p. 95.

20 July 1786. Frederick PENNINGTON and Ann Williamson. Sur. William Graves. Married 27 July by Rev. John Meglamore. p. 43.

8 December 1801. James PENNINGTON and Polly Loftin. Sur. James C. Bailey. Wit: Winfield Pennington. p. 103.

20 December 1786. John PENNINGTON and Sally Graves. Married 26 December by Rev. John Meglamore. Sur. David Graves. p. 45.

20 July 1769. Marcus PENNINGTON and Ann Graves, dau. Solomon Graves who is surety. p. 13.

6 November 1810. Thomas PENNINGTON and Mary Adkins, dau. Willis Adkins. Sur. Benjamin Marable. Wit: Alexander Raney and Solomon Graves. p. 137.

7 March 1810. Stephen PEPPER and Lucy Bailey, dau. Phillip Bailey. Sur. Edmund Bailey. p. 135.

21 December 1795. Robert PERSONS and Catharine Stacy. Sur. Nicholas Stacy. p. 79. See Robert Parsons.

29 March 1768. James PETERS and Lucy Parker, infant (under age), dau. William Parker. James infant (under age), son of Thomas Peters. Sur. William Hines. Wit: William Parker, Jr. p. 12.

----- 1791. William PETERS and Peggy Loftin. Married by Rev. John Meglamore. Ministers' Returns p. 265.

21 April 1764. John PETERSON and Elizabeth Briggs, dau. George Briggs. John Peterson of Brunswick County. Sur. James Maclin, Jr. p. 8.

15 June 1775. Thomas PETERSON and Elizabeth Claiborne, dau. Col. Augustine Claiborne. Sur. Buller Claiborne. p. 21.

------ 1801. ----- PETERSON and Dolly Sturdivant. Married by Rev. Stith Parham. Ministers' Returns p. 277.

20 September 1785. John PETTIPOOL and Rebecca Wilkerson, widow. Sur. Thomas Hardaway. p. 39.

17 November 1785. Seth PETTIPOOL and Lucrecy Winfield, consent of Peter Winfield. Sur. David Mason. Wit: Henry Jones. p. 40.

6 September 1792. Benjamin PETTWAY and Levina Harwood. Sur. Allen Jones. p. 68.

28 January 1771. Edward PETTWAY, Jr. and Susanna Pettway. Edward Pettway, Jr. of Brunswick County. Sur. Edward Pettway. Wit: Billey Claiborne. p. 14.

15 February 1808. Edwin PETTWAY and Winny Pair. Sur. William Thornton. p. 128.

20 November 1767. Hinchia PETTWAY and Mary Parker, consent of John Jones. Wit: Herbert Claiborne. Sur. David Mason. Wit: James Jones, Joel Tucker and William Parham. p. 11.

24 October 1765. John PETTWAY and Fanny Biggins, dau. Sarah Biggins. Sur. William Pettway, Jr. Wit: Elizabeth Weeks. p. 9.

5 January 1760. Robert PETTWAY and Phoebe Pettway, dau. Edward Pettway who is surety. p. 5.

16 September 1790. Robert PETTWAY and Ann Bell Harwood, ward of Robert Jones. Married 18 September by Rev. John Meglamore. Sur. John Bell. p. 61.

26 September 1801. Robert PETTWAY and Nancy Eckols. Sur. William Eckols. p. 102.

17 July 1805. William PETTWAY and Franky Mitchell. Sur. Thomas Mitchell. p. 118.

24 February 1762. Hartwell PHILIPS and Jane Hancock, dau. John Hancock who consents. Hartwell Philips of Surry County. Sur. Benjamin Clary. p. 6.

1 March 1790. Edwin PHILLIPS and Susanna Clary, dau. Mary Clary. Sur. James Clary. p. 59.

1 January 1789. Mark PHILLIPS and Lucy Jordan. Married 3 January by Rev. John Easter. Sur. Jesse Lane. p. 53.

13 April 1789. Benjamin PHIPPS and Ruth Hays. Married 21 April by Rev. John Meglamore. Sur. Robert Bonds. p. 55.

10 September 1799. John PHIPPS and Nancy Long. Sur. James Hogwood. p. 94.

23 March 1793. Jordan PHIPPS and Penelope McCullock. Sur. John Underwood. p. 71.

15 December 1790. Richardson PHIPPS and Fanney Newsom. Sur. Eldridge Newsom. p. 61.

14 November 1791. Micajah PLEASANTS and Dolly Pleasants, dau. William Pleasants. Sur. Thomas Pleasants. p. 64.

19 February 1791. William PLEASANTS and Amelia Judkins. Sur. Thomas Holloway. p. 63.

2 February 1797. William PLEASANTS and Fathy Andrews, consent of Henry and Jane Andrews. Married 4 February by Rev. Drewry Lane. Sur. Buford Pleasants. Wit: Thomas and Burwell Pleasants. p. 85.

22 March 1802. Albridgton POPE and Sally Birdsong, dau. William Birdsong who is surety. Wit: Nancy Owen. Married 25 March by Rev. Drewry Lane. p. 106.

9 March 1789. Henry PORCH and Sarah Wrenn. Married 12 March by Rev. John Easter. Sur. Henry Moss. p. 55.

4 December 1810. James PORCH and Sally Horn. Sur. William Thomas. p. 137.

2 November 1789. Seth PORCH and Nancy Pair. Married 15 December by Rev. Henry Moss. Sur. Marcus Zills. p. 57.

6 January 1804. Thomas PORCH and Patsey Booth. Sur. Nathaniel Davis. p. 113.

31 July 1801. William PORCH and Polly Carrell. Sur. Samuel Smith. p. 102.

20 April 1801. Daniel PORTER and Polly Ellis, dau. Amy Ellis. Sur. Henry Parsons. p. 101.

10 December 1796. Donaldson POTTER and Catharine Ellis. Married 22 December by Rev. Drewry Lane. Sur. Robert Ellis. p. 84.

20 December 1808. Charles POTTS and Patsy Land. Married 22 December by Rev. Drewry Lane. Sur. John Chappell. p. 130.

28 August 1807. Thomas POTTS and Lucy Graves, dau. David Graves. Married 3 September by Rev. James Rogers. Sur. Robert Moore. p. 126.

3 May 1798. James POWELL and Rebeckah Bell, consent of Silvanus Bell. Sur. Richard Rose. p. 90.

6 September 1780. John POWELL and Boys Gee. Sur. Joesph Heath, Jr. Wit: George Rives. p. 26.

3 January 1805. Ludwell POWELL and Elizabeth Parham. Married 10 January by Rev. James Rogers. Sur. Lewis Parham. p. 116.

4 February 1796. Robert POWELL and Mary Lucas Robertson (Robinson), ward of Stith Parham. Married 18 February by Rev. Stith Parham. Sur. William Pettway. p. 80.

29 June 1795. Nicholas PRESSON and Permelia Smith. Sur. Richard Presson. p. 77.

7 April 1810. Nicholas PRESSON and Elizabeth Chappell. Sur. James Chappell, Sr. p. 135.

7 January 1795. Richard PRESSON and Nancy Carrell, dau. William Carrell, Sr. who is surety. p. 76.

21 December 1801. Thomas L. PRESSON and Mary Ellis. Married 24 December by Rev. Drewry Lane. Sur. Richard Presson. p. 104.

15 April 1784. Samuel PRETLOW and Nancy Thomas. Samuel Pretlow of Surry County, ward of B. Bailey. Sur. Michael Blow. Wit: William Bailey and Edward Bailey. p. 35.

10 December 1810. Samuel PRETLOW and Edna Bailey. Married 12 December by Rev. Drewry Lane. Sur. John Nicholson. Wit: Gulie Bailey. p. 137.

27 November 1757. Hallcott PRIDE and Mary Briggs, dau. Capt. Howell Briggs. Sur. Henry Woodcock of Sussex. Hallcott Pride of Dinwiddie County. p. 3.

4 November 1791. John PRINCE and Martha Phipps. Sur. William Prince. p. 64.

23 October 1789. Joseph PRINCE and Priscilla Adams. Married 3 November by Rev. John Meglamore. Sur. John Prince. p. 57.

5 July 1798. William PRINCE and Patsy Mason. Sur. Joseph Prince. p. 91.

16 December 1773. John PRITCHARD and Elizabeth Tharp, dau. Joseph Tharp. Sur. Nathaniel Wyche. p. 17.

17 April 1782. Micajah PROCTOR and Suffiah Rodgers, dau. David and Jane Rodgers. Sur. William Ellis. Wit: Stephen Andrews. p. 30.

21 June 1791. William PULLEN and Mason Fort. Sur. William Clanton. Married by Rev. William Brown. p. 63.

7 November 1786. David PUTNEY and Mary Chapman Wyche, dau. Nathaniel Wyche, deceased, and Mary Wyche. Sur. Robert Land. p. 44.

10 February 1778. Hinchia RACHEL and Jemima Atkinson, dau. Amos Atkinson of North Carolina. Sur. Nathaniel Newsum. Wit: William Renn. p. 23.

2 November 1792. Jarrad RACHEL and Viny Davis. Sur. Matthew Davis. p. 69. See Jarrad Rochel.

4 April 1796. Charles RAILEY and Polly Mayo. Sur. Martin Railey.
Wit: John Martin. p. 81.

3 May 1756. Frederick RAINES and Frances Wyche, dau. James Wyche,
deceased, and ward of William Johnson. Frederick son of Richard
Raines of Prince George County. Sur. Thomas Young. Wit: Isham
Browder, Peter Jones and Nathaniel Raines. p. 2.

17 October 1776. Hartwell RAINES and Elizabeth Wyche, dau. James
Wyche, deceased. Sur. James Jones. p. 21.

18 July 1800. Nathaniel RAINES and Elizabeth Johnson, ward of
Thomas Dunn. Sur. George Rives. p. 97.

5 October 1762. John RAINES and Amy Mitchell, widow. Sur. Nathaniel
Mitchell. p. 7.

21 April 1774. John RAINES, Jr. and Ann Webb, dau. Robert Webb,
deceased. p. 18.

26 April 1809. Nathaniel RAINES and Susanna Jones. Married 27
April by Rev. James Rogers. Sur. Samuel L. Raines. p. 133.

20 December 1808. Alexander RAINEY and Ann Graves, dau. David
Graves. Returned 12 Jan. 1809, by Rev. James Rogers. Sur. Soloman
Graves. p. 130.

2 March 1809. Daniel RAINEY and Priscilla Brunt. Sur. James
Malone. p. 132.

3 April 1800. James RAINEY and Martha Parham. Sur. William
Parham. p. 96.

22 April 1801. John RAINEY and Phebe Chappell, dau. Thomas
Chappell. Sur. Thomas Shands. Wit: Peter Rainey and William
Malone. Married by Rev. Stith Parham. p. 101.

5 December 1799. William RAINEY and Betsy Bobbitt. Married 19
December by Rev. Stith Parham. Sur. John Bobbitt. p. 95.
See William Raney.

30 July 1773. Peter RANDALL and Frances Parham, dau. James
Parham. Sur. Matthew Parham. Wit: Isham Bilbry. p. 17.

10 November 1801. George RANDOLPH and Lucretia Tucker Chappell,
dau. Thomas Chappell. Sur. Thomas Malone. Wit: Thomas Shands,
John Ivie and William Malone. p. 103.

19 December 1799. William RANEY and Elizabeth Bobbitt. Married
by Rev. Stith Parham. Ministers' Returns p. 273. See William
Rainey.

6 September 1792. John RAWLINGS and Mary Abernathy. Married 27
September by Rev. William Brown. Sur. James Abernathy. p. 68.

------- 1791. Richard RAWLINGS and Rebecca Weaver. Married by
Rev. William Brown. Ministers' Returns p. 266. See Richard
Rollings.

27 September 1809. Eldridge RAY and Polly Hogwood, dau. Edith
Hogwood. Returned 28 November by Rev. James Rogers. Sur. Carter
Hogwood. p. 133.

27 June 1801. Robert RAY and Mary Ann Underhill. Sur. William
Edwards. p. 101.

17 February 1788. Joel READING and Martha Batts. Married by Rev.
Jesse Lee. Ministers' Returns p. 261. See Joel Redding.

1 September 1796. Joel READING and Martha Halcome. Sur. Thomas
Mitchell. Wit: Adam Lee and John Reading. p. 83.

9 Febuary 1788. Joel REDDING and Martha Batts. Married 17 February
by Rev. Jesse Lee. Sur. Frederick Batts. Wit: John Redding.
p. 50. See Joel Reading.

20 December 1787. Anderson REDING and Elisha Parham, dau. Haddon
Parham. Sur. Joel Reding. Wit: John Biggins. p. 49.

22 January 1784. Charles REDING and Edy Hobbs. Married by Rev.
John Meglamore. Ministers' Returns p. 323.

19 December 1808. Edward REESE and Polly W. Gilliam. Married
22 December by Rev. Robert Murrell, Sr. of Southampton County.
Sur. William Gilliam. p. 130.

4 June 1791. Jacob REESE and Dyaney (Diana?) Meacham. Sur.
John Simmons Meacham. p. 63.

19 January 1786. John REESE and Rebeccah Collier. Sur. Samson
Collier. Returned 23 February by Rev. John Meglamore. p. 41.

16 February 1799. Lewis REESE and Nancy Harwood. Married 17
February by Rev. Stith Parham. Sur. Partain Bullock. Wit: James
McLemore. p. 93.

Returned February 1793. Bates RENN and Clarsa Jones. Married
by Rev. George Parham. Ministers' Returns p. 268.

24 Marvh 1768. Joseph RENN and Ann Zills, widow. Sur. Thomas
Renn. Wit: William Mason. p. 12.

11 June 1789. Joseph RENN and Sarah Mangum, dau. Samuel Mangum.
Sur. William Clanton. p. 56.

14 May 1789. Matthew REVILL and Martha Newsom. Married 20 May by Rev. John Meglamore. Sur. Richardson Phipps. p. 56.

26 January 1775. Jordan RICHARDSON and Elizabeth Mason, dau. Col. David Mason. Sur. Littleberry Mason. p. 20.

18 December 1809. Thomas RICHARDSON and Sally U. Gary, dau. Benjamin Gary. Sur. Peyton Underhill. p. 134.

5 April 1792. William RICHARDSON and Mary Rose. Married 22 April by Rev. Henry Moss. Sur. John Massenburg. p. 67.

17 December 1796. William RICHARDSON and Frances Briggs. Married 24 December by Rev. Drewry Lane. Sur. Stephen Andrews. p. 85.

12 February 1763. Timothy RIEVES and Catherine Barker, widow of Henry Barker. Sur. William Chamblis. p. 7.

12 December 1788. Robert RIVERS, Jr. and Nancy Eldridge, consent of John Massenburt. Sur. David Mason. p. 53. See Robert Rives.

16 December 1773. William RIVERS and Elizabeth Vaughan, dau. Thomas Vaughan. p. 18. See William Rives.

2 July 1759. Christopher RIVES and Elizabeth Mason. Sur. John Mason. p. 5.

9 January 1762. George RIVES and Sarah Eldridge, dau. Thomas Eldridge, deceased. Sur. William Eldridge. p. 6.

25 November 1795. George RIVES and Martha Goodwyn, dau. Joseph Goodwyn, Sr. Sur. Thomas E. Rives. Wit: Anthony Rives and Isaac Oliver. p. 79.

18 December 1788. Robert RIVES and Ann Eldridge. Married by Rev. John Easter. Ministers' Returns p. 262. See Robert Rivers.

8 February 1773. Timothy RIVES and Martha Binns. Sur. John Cargill. Wit: Lucy Cargill. p. 17.

4 February 1780. Timothy RIVES and Rebecca Mason. Sur. John Mason. p. 25.

16 December 1773. William RIVES and Elizabeth Vaughan, dau. Thomas Vaughan. p. 18. See William Rivers.

19 January 1775. William RIVES and Jemima Heath, dau. William Heath. William Rives of Prince George County. Sr. Nathan Heath. Wit: Seth Heath. p. 20.

18 September 1782. Benjamin ROBERTS and Catharine Jones. Sur. James Boisseau. p. 31.

28 May 1802. Wilbert ROBERTS and Anne Nicholson. Married 2 June by Rev. Drewry Lane. p. 107.

6 March 1804. James ROBERTSON and Frances Cain. Sur. Curtis Winfield. p. 114.

19 July 1800. John ROBERTSON and Sally Rainey. Sur. Peter Rainey. p. 97.

2 January 1783. Randal ROBERTSON and Amey Malone, widow. Sur. John Powell. p. 32.

21 August 1783. John Crew ROBINSON and Rebekah Jarratt, widow of Jesse Jarratt. Sur. Gray Judkins. p. 33.

7 January 1808. William ROBINSON and Rebecca Bonner Welborne. Sur. William Welborne. p. 127.

22 November 1792. Jarrad ROCHEL and Viney Davis. Married by Rev. William Brown. Ministers' Returns p. 267. See Jarrad Rachel.

-- October 1796. Charles ROCKLEY and Polly Mays. Married by Rev. George Parham. Ministers' Returns p. 270.

31 July 1793. Collin RODGERS and Elizabeth Barker. Sur. Charles Briggs, Jr. Married 8 August by Rev. Drewry Lane. p. 71.

17 August 1786. Robert ROE and Ann Jennings. Sur. Peter Jennings. p. 43.

4 April 1795. Robert ROE and Anne Bains. Sur. George Dillard. p. 77.

7 November 1793. Allen ROGERS and Mary H. Lane. Married 14 November by Rev. Drewry Lane. Sur. Joseph Rosser. p. 72.

8 August 1793. Collin ROGERS and Elizabeth Barker. Married by Rev. Drewry Lane. Ministers' Returns p. 268.

17 April 1800. James ROGERS and Elizabeth Graves, dau. William Graves. Married 19 April by Rev. Drewry Lane. Sur. Samuel Risher. p. 97.

27 January 1784. Joshua ROLAND and Ann Whitehead. Married by Rev. John Meglamore. Ministers' Returns p. 323.

7 April 1806. Henry ROLLINGS and Lurana Tuder. Married 16 April by Rev. James Rogers. Sur. Jesse Tudor. p. 120.

7 December 1791. Richard ROLLINGS and Rebecca Weaver. Sur. Benjamin Hay. p. 65. See Richard Rawlings.

20 December 1786. Elijah ROSE and Elizabeth Roland. Sur. Frederick Northcross. Married 26 December by Rev. John Meglamore who says Elisha Rose. p. 45.

7 September 1796. Robert ROSE and Dorothy Andrews. Sur. George Moseley. p. 83.

15 November 1790. James ROWLAND and Betsey Felts. Married 9 December by Rev. George Mason. Sur. Augustine Felts. Ministers' Returns say Elizabeth Felts. p. 61.

3 December 1799. John ROWLAND and Elizabeth Rowland. Sur. Robert Owen. p. 95.

4 January 1810. Joseph ROWLAND and Susan Bonds. Sur. Joseph Wrenn. p. 135.

3 December 1807. Thomas ROWLAND and Elizabeth Davis, dau. Lucy Davis. Sur. Thomas Wilkinson. Married by Rev. James Gibbons. p. 126.

9 April 1762. William RUFFIN and Sarah Hill, dau. Richard Hill who is surety. William Ruffin of Edgcomb County North Carolina. Wit: Charles Harrison. p. 6.

19 April 1780. Richard RUSSELL and Lucy Carter, dau. Joseph Carter. Richard Russell ward of Peter Williams of Prince George County. Sur. William Presley Claiborne. Wit: William Horton. p. 26.

6 February 1802. John SALLE and Betsey Moody. Sur. Burwell Bacon. Wit: Thompson Blunt. p. 105.

18 July 1755. John SAMMON and Lucy Seat, dau. Robert Seat. Sur. Nathaniel Jonson. p. 1. See John Samons.

16 December 1803. Braxton SAMMONS and Polly Hern. Returned 17 January 1804 by Rev. Robert Murrell, Sr. of Southampton County. Sur. James Hubbard. p. 113.

3 November 1791. Groves SAMMONS and Sarah Sledge. Sur. Osmond Dunn. Wit: James Sammons. Married by Rev. William Brown. p. 64.

13 December 1796. Hansel SAMMONS and Rebecca Barker. Sur. Groves Sammons. p. 85.

31 August 1801. Hansel SAMMONS and Nancy Mannery, dau. John Mannery. Sur. James Sammons. Wit: James Manery. p. 102.

11 May 1803. James SAMMONS and Sally Hearn. Sur. Henry Tudor, Jr. p. 111.

10 October 1795. Samuel SAMMONS and Sarah Morgan. Sur. Balaam Hay. p. 78.

26 July 1790. Thomas SAMMONS and Elizabeth Morgan. Married 4 August by Rev. John Meglamore. Sur. Thomas Sledge. p. 60.

18 July 1755. John SAMONS and Lucy Seat, dau. Robert Seat. Sur. Nathaniel Jonaon. p. 1. See John Sammon.

25 October 1765. Thomas Sanders and Ann Harper, widow. Sur. John Bonner. p. 9.

21 December 1809. James SCAMMELL and Lucy Clements. Married 27 December by Rev. James Rogers. Sur. Peter Booth. p. 135.

13 January 1808. Collin SCARBROUGH and Susan Dunn. Married 21 January by Rev. Robert Murrell, Sr. of Southampton County. Sur. Henry Tudor, Jr. p. 127.

1 September 1808. Benjamin SCOGGIN and Polly Perkins. Sur. Daniel Nives. p. 129.

20 November 1788. William SCOGGIN and Celia Cotton. Sur. John McKinney. p. 52.

21 February 1789. Thomas E. SCOTT and Nancy Blow, dau. Henry Blow. Sur. Charles Briggs, Jr. p. 55.

9 March 1793. Benjamin SEABORNE and Fanny Mosely. Sur. Silas Long. Wit: Sampson Mosely. p. 71.

16 April 1794. Frederick SEABORNE and Dolly Sands, consent of William Tomlinson. Married 19 April by Rev. William Brown. Sur. Archibald Parker. p. 74.

6 May 1790. Howell SEABORNE and Elizabeth Arnold Hudson. Sur. John Hudson. Married by Rev. John Mason. p. 60.

30 October 1782. William SEARES and Mildred Smith, dau. Arthur Smith. Sur. John Cocke. Wit: F. Smith, Harrod Comer and William Marriott. p. 31.

------- 1791. Joseph SEAT and Martha Bottom. Married by Rev. John Meglamore. Ministers' Returns p. 265. See Josiah Seat.

5 February 1791. Josiah SEAT and Martha Bottom, dau. William Bottom who is surety. p. 62. See Joseph Seat.

17 December 1764. John SHANDS and Phebe Shands, dau. William
and Priscilla Shands. Sur. William Rives. Wit: Augustine Shands.
p. 9.

2 June 1779. William SHANDS and Lucy Oliver, dau. William Oliver.
Sur. Augustine Shands. p. 24.

25 January 1773. Burwell SHARP and Mary Gibbons, age 24, born
in York County, dau. John Gibbons, deceased and sister and ward
of Thomas Gibbons who is surety. Wit: George Williams, Jr. p. 16.

2 September 1803. Philips SHELLY and Betsy Cook. p. 112.

1 November 1788. Thomas SHORE and Sarah Belsches. Thomas Shore
of Petersburg. Sur. Hugh Belsches. Wit: Henry Shore. p. 52.

2 May 1806. Archibald SHUFFIELD and Lucrecy Cooper, dau. James
Cooper. Sur. Thomas Cooper. p. 120.

15 April 1779. John SIMMONS and Lucretia Jones. Sur. Mordecai
Jones. p. 24.

17 February 1769. Thomas SISSON and Martha Parker, dau. William
Parker, deceased and ward of William Hines. Thomas Sisson of
Brunswick County. Sur. James Peters. Wit: Eldridge Clack. p. 12.

26 October 1793. John SLEDGE and Cinthia Sammons. Married 6
November by Rev. William Brown. Sur. James Sammons. p. 72.

25 October 1802. Parrot SLEDGE and Betsy Munds. Married 27
October by Rev. James Rogers. Sur. John Bush. p. 108.

2 February 1796. Sterling SLEDGE and Polly Wiggins. Sur. Wilson
Wi-gins. p. 80.

2 April 1795. Allen SMITH and Silvyer Felts. Sur. Weathers Adams.
p. 77.

21 December 1780. Benjamin SMITH and Jane Briggs. Sur. Peter
Jones. p. 27.

11 December 1790. Benjamin SMITH and Sarah Bendall. Married
14 December by Rev. Henry Moss. Sur. Isaac Bendall. p. 61.

14 March 1796. Charles SMITH and Susanna Williamson, consent of
Buckner Lanier (her step-father). Sur. James Williamson. p. 81.

18 September 1799. Charles SMITH and Martha Chambliss, dau.
James Chambliss. Returned 3 October by Rev. Stith Parham. Sur.
Edward Pennington. p. 94.

9 April 1791. Frederick SMITH and Elizabeth Ambruss (Ambrose).
Married by Rev. Jesse Lee. Ministers' Returns p. 264.

31 March 1807. George SMITH and Sally Hanson Garrettson. Married
15 April by Rev. James Rogers. Sur. William Parham. p. 124.

23 March 1803. Holmes B. SMITH and Ann M. Partridge. Married
24 March by Rev. Drewry Lane. Sur. Robert Jones. p. 110.

6 September 1810. James SMITH and Elizabeth Heath. Sur. Thomas
Dunn. p. 136.

27 November 1799. John SMITH and Elizabeth Fogg. Married 28
November by Rev. Stith Parham. Sur. Thomas Chambliss. p. 95.

12 October 1802. John SMITH and Nancy Goodwin. Sur. George
Goodwin. p. 108.

7 December 1797. Joshua SMITH and Susanna J. Marks. Sur. Robert
Wrenn. p. 87.

19 December 1807. Larkin SMITH and Mary G. Parsons. Sur. Robert
Parsons. p. 126.

12 August 1767. Lawrence SMITH and Mary Briggs, widow. Sur.
William Wilcox. p. 11.

7 November 1799. Ned SMITH and Mary Huson, dau. Ann Huson. Ned
Smith of Dinwiddie County. Returned 28 November by Rev. Stith
Parham. Sur. Robert Nicholson. p. 94.

12 August 1784. Richard SMITH, Jr. and Sylvia Cotton, dau.
William Cotton. Sur. Julius Hite. Wit: David Cotton. p. 35.

11 November 1786. Samuel SMITH and Rachel Carrol, dau. William
Carrol. Sur. James Alsabrook Wrenn. Wit: James Wrenn, Rebecca
White and John Ellis. Married 16 November by Rev. John Meglamore.
p. 43.

15 February 1792. Samuel SMITH and Tempey Edmunds. Married 16
February by Rev. Drewry Lane. Sur. William Chappell. p. 66.

25 November 1808. Samuel SMITH and Judith Sykes. Sur. Charles
Potts. p. 130.

18 August 1760. Holman SOUTHALL and Elizabeth Dancy, dau. William
Dancy. Sur. Hugh Belscher. p. 5.

20 December 1790. Charles SOUTHWARD and Rebecca Rawlings.
Married 27 December by Rev. John Meglamore. Sur. Jonathan Harrup.
Wit: M. W. Hancock. p. 62.

4 December 1800. Absalom SPAIN and Nancy Parham. Sur. Thomas
Malone. Wit: Thomas Green. Married by Rev. Stith Parham. p. 99.

14 May 1782. Claiborne SPAIN and Frances Threeweeks. Married by
Rev. John Meglamore. Ministers' Returns p. 257.

27 December 1803. Daniel SPAIN and Sally Thomas. Sur. James
Thomas. p. 113.

1 October 1790. Ezekiah SPAIN and Sally Adkins, dau. Mrs. Ann
T. Witts. Ezekiah son of Abigail Spain. Sur. James Spain. Married
by Rev. George Parham. p. 61.

14 December 1790. James SPAIN and Lucretia Stewart (widow).
James son of James Spain, Sr. Sur. William Spain. p. 61.

23 December 1806. John SPAIN and Rebecca Roe. Married 24
December by Rev. James Rogers. Sur. Benjamin Roe. p. 123.

14 December 1802. Thomas SPAIN and Elizabeth Whitehead, dau.
Isham Whitehead. Married 15 December by Rev. James Rogers. Sur.
Edmund Whitehead. p. 109.

17 December 1791. William Hill SPAIN and Amy Gilliam Spain, dau.
James Spain, Sr. who is surety. Wit: James Spain, Jr. William
Hill Spain son of William Spain. Married by Rev. William Brown.
p. 65.

3 December 1807. John SPENCER and Mary Mason. Sur. William Parham.
Married by Rev. James Gibbons. p. 126.

3 October 1793. Thomas SPENCER and Mary Mason, dau. Mary Mason.
Married 10 October by Rev. William Brown. Sur. John P. Pettway.
Wit: William Massenburg. p. 72.

23 April 1798. Charles SPIRES and Peggy Horn. Sur. John
Atkinson. p. 89.

14 August 1809. Frederick SPIRES and Phebe Rachell, dau. Jarratt
Rachell. Sur. Adam Spires. Wit: Lewis Parham. p. 133.

16 August 1787. Benjamin STACY and Lucy Cooper. Sur. Benjamin
Cooper. p. 48.

6 November 1797. Edmund STACY and Rebecca Harrison. Married 9
November by Rev. Drewry Lane. Sur. Cary Cotton. p. 87.

24 November 1797. William STACY and Susan Watson. Married 30
November by Rev. Drewry Lane. Sur. William Cotton. p. 87.

14 October 1802. William A. STACY and Jinsey Stratson. Sur.
Nicholas Stacy. p. 108.

13 February 1782. David STAFFORD and Elizabeth Spain. Married by Rev. John Meglamore. Ministers' Returns p. 257.

6 April 1805. Daniel STANTON and Mary Newby. Sur. Thomas D. Heath. p. 117.

4 November 1797. Samuel STANTON and Rachel Nicholson. Married by Rev. Drewry Lane. Ministers' Returns p. 271.

22 December 1790. Ransom STOKES and Sally Cocks. Sur. George Dowdy. p. 62.

5 January 1798. Richard STOKES and Rebecca Partain. Married 6 January by Rev. Henry Moss. Sur. Edmund Hobbs. p. 88.

14 September 1796. William STOKES and Martha Wyche, dau. Mary Wyche. Sur. Braxton Robertson. Wit: Nathaniel Wyche. p. 83.

18 October 1777. Dr. Alexander Glass STRACHEN (Straughn) and Lucy Pride, ward of Colin Campbell of Surry County. Dr. Straughn of Prince George County. Sur. John Nelson, Jr. p. 23.

5 February 1795. Thomas STUART and Winifred Atkins. Sur. Moses Brown. p. 76.

29 January 1792. Anthony STURDIVANT and Martha Hall King, consent of Sally King. Sur. Benjamin Crews. Married by Rev. George Parham. p. 66.

3 January 1793. Benjamin STURDIVANT and Elizabeth Whitfield, dau. Thomas Whitfield. Married 20 January by Rev. Henry Moss. Sur. James Knight. p. 70.

21 December 1784. Charles STURDIVANT and Martha Knight. Married by Rev. John Meglamore. Ministers' Returns p. 323.

5 January 1797. Charles W. STURDIVANT and Sally Wynne. Sur. Benjanin Sturdivant. Wit: Moses Knight, Jr. Married by Rev. Henry Moss.. p. 85.

20 November 1788. Hollom STURDIVANT, Jr. and Drusilla Hobbs. Married 22 November by Rev. Jesse Lee. Sur. Thomas Whitfield. p. 52.

28 December 1773. John STURDIVANT, Jr. and Rebecca Robinson, age 23, dau. George Robinson, deceased, and Mary Robinson. p. 18.

13 October 1781. John STURDIVANT and Selah Hobbs. Married by Rev. John Meglamore. Ministers' Returns p. 257.

19 December 1787. Mathew STURDIVANT and Patsy Tomlinson, consent of Alexander Tomlinson. Sur. William Whitfield. p. 49.

6 August 1795. Matthew STURDIVANT and Frances Tomlinson, consent of Thomas Bailey. Sur. William Whitfield. Married by Rev. Henry Moss. p. 78.

9 April 1798. Matthew STURDIVANT and Frances Wynne. Sur. William Wynne. Married by Rev. Henry Moss. p. 89.

6 February 1787. Robert STURDIVANT and Anne Sturdivant, dau. Thomas Sturdivant. p. 46.

1 May 1788. Robert STURDIVANT and Mary Jones. Sur. William Horn. p. 51.

4 January 1793. Robert STURDIVANT and Rebecca Sledge, dau. Thomas Sledge. Sur. Benjamin Sturdivant. Married by Rev. George Parham. p. 70.

27 December 1784. Thomas STURDIVANT and Elizabeth Knight. Married by Rev. John Meglamore. Ministers' Returns p. 323.

2 February 1805. James SYKES and Nancy Jones, ward of James Davis. Sur. Herod Birt. Wit: Elizabeth Jones. p. 117.

15 December 1786. Nathan TANNER and Mary Mitchell. Sur. Thomas Huson. Wit: John Mitchell, Jacob Mitchell and William Rives. p. 44.

12 May 1787. Seth TANNER and Sally Kelley, dau. John Kelley. Married 4 June by Rev. John Meglamore. Sur. John Kelly, Jr. p. 47.

30 January 1773. Robert TATUM and Amy Gee, dau. Charles Gee. Robert son of Robert Tatum of Prince George County, deceased. Sur. David Lessenberry. Wit: William Rives. p. 16.

18 September 1782. James TAYLOR and Elizabeth McCormick, age near 30. Sur. Michael Booth. Wit: Joel Epps. p. 31.

26 February 1798. Burwell TEMPLE and Polly Simmons. Married by Rev. Augustine Heath. Ministers' Returns p. 272.

7 September 1797. Burwell TEMPLE and Polly Simmons Adkins. Sur. Willis Adkins. p. 85.

22 March 1771. John TEWEL and Mary Mason, dau. Isaac Mason, deceased. Sur. John Rives. p. 14. See John Tuel.

8 December 1779. Benjamin THOMAS and Rebecca Johnson, infant (under age), dau. Lewis Johnson. Benjamin Thomas of North Carolina. Sur. Sylvanus Bell. Wit: William Presley Claiborne and Benjamin Johnson. p. 25.

20 October 1807. James THOMAS and Elizabeth Horn. Married 5 November by Rev. James Rogers. Sur. William Whitehead. p. 126.

2 April 1807. Lewis THOMAS and Catherine Pate. Married 16 April by Rev. Robert Murrell, Sr. of Southampton Co. Sur. James Thomas. p. 124.

8 September 1788. William THOMPSON and Lucy Herbert Cocke. Sur. Thomas Claiborne. p. 51.

4 August 1800. William THOMPSON and Rebecca Beard. Sur. Daniel Grant. p. 97.

30 January 1809. William THORNTON and Mary Parham. Sur. William H. Comann. Married 2 February by Rev. James Rogers. p. 131.

1 August 1801. Aaron THORP and Polly Cooper. Married 9 August by Rev. William Hargrave. Sur. Herbert Mason. p. 102.

10 February 1755. William THWEATT and Jane Parham, dau. Ephraim Parham. Sur. James Thweatts. p. 1.

19 December 1782. David THWEAT and Rebecca Gee, widow. David Thweat of Dinwiddie County. Sur. Solomon Graves. p. 31.

16 March 1784. Drury THWEAT and Selah Smith, dau. Isham Smith. Sur. Peter Cain. Wit: John Freeman. p. 34.

1 October 1801. Drury TILLER and Sally Knight. Sur. Henry Knight. p. 102.

15 November 1791. Hardah TOMLINSON and Lizza Hobbs. Married 17 November by Rev. Henry Moss. Sur. Thomas Ellis. p. 65.

17 October 1792. James TOMLINSON and Nancy Hobbs. Sur. Joshua Moss. Married by Rev. Henry Moss. p. 68.

6 January 1789. John TOMLINSON and Sarah Stewart, dau. Richard Stewart. Sur. William Tomlinson. Wit: John Cross. p. 54.

18 April 1809. Nathaniel TOMLINSON and Sally Neblett, dau. Polly Neblett. Married 27 April by Rev. James Rogers. Sur. Edwin Pettway. p. 132.

1 November 1783. Richard TOMLINSON and Sally Ray. Sur. William Tomlinson. Married by Rev. John Meglamore. p. 33.

30 December 1803. Richard TOMLINSON and Mary Hix. Sur. Thomas Presson. p. 113.

3 May 1804. Richard TOMPKINS and Mary Hicks. Married by Rev. Joseph Hill. Ministers' Returns p. 278.

1 December 1803. Britain TRAVIS and Polly Johnson, dau. Collins Johnson. Married 22 December by Rev. James Rogers. Sur. Burwell Gilliam. p. 112.

7 November 1795. Charles TRAVIS and Temperance Wilborne, consent of John Wilborn. Sur. Etheldred Evans. p. 79.

10 February 1789. Pyland TRAVIS and Lucy Hargrave, dau. Letice Hargrave. Sur. Drury Lane. p. 55.

4 April 1803. John TREZVANT and Nancy Bell, dau. Silvanus Bell. Sur. John Green. p. 110.

7 November 1794. Richard TROUBLEFIELD and Martha Eckols. Sur. Reuben Jackson. p. 75.

28 November 1803. Richard TROUBLEFIELD and Tabitha Heath. Sur. William Jackson. Wit: Charles Raines. p. 112.

8 March 1800. Biggins TUCKER and Jackey Harrison, dau. Alexander Harrison. Sur. Thomas Hobbs. p. 96.

24 November 1759. David TUCKER and Athaliah Kezia Hunt, widow. Sur. Thomas Goodwyn. p. 5.

21 November 1783. Paschal TUCKER and Mary Pennington. Married by Rev. John Meglamore. Ministers' Returns p. 322.

2 September 1772. Robert TUCKER and Mary Ann Parham. Robert Tucker of Prince George County. Sur. Stith Parham. Wit: Samuel Todd. p. 16. Double wedding: See Stith Parham.

19 May 1795. Henry TUDER and Winny Sammons. Sur. Richard Parker. Wit: William Lane. p. 77.

4 December 1806. Landon TUDER and Rebecca Tuder, dau. Henry Tuder, Jr. Married 11 December by Rev. James Rogers. Sur. Ransome Hogwood. p. 122.

21 November 1783. Henry TUDOR and Crecy Adams. Married by Rev. John Meglamore. Ministers' Returns p. 322.

22 March 1771. John TUEL and Mary Mason, dau. Isaac Mason, deceased. Sur. John Rives. p. 14. See John Tewell.

26 March 1802. Benjamin TURNER and Martha Mitchell. Sur. Reaps. Mitchell. p. 106.

3 February 1791. Daniel TURNER and Christian Burges. Sur. Howell Jones. p. 62.

24 January 1786. James TURNER and Frances Betts. Married by
Rev. John Meglamore. Ministers' Returns p. 258.

22 December 1800. William TURNER and Betsey Raines, dau. Charles
Raines. Sur. Edward Butler. p. 99.

14 December 1801. William TURNER and Avarilla Kitchen. Married
17 December by Rev. Drewry Lane. Sur. Drury Betts. p. 104.

17 January 1803. Joseph TYUS and Elizabeth Andrews, dau. Mrs.
-------- Andrews. Sur. Ely Williams. p. 109.

1 January 1807. Pinkey TYUS and Polly Niblett. Married 8 January
by Rev. James Rogers. Sur. Thomas Atkinson. p. 123.

10 December 1788. Thomas TYUS and Nancy Hall, dau. James Hall.
Married 11 December by Rev. John Easter. Sur. William Hall. p. 53.

14 March 1805. Thomas TYUS and Sally Malone. Married by Rev.
John N. Smith. Ministers' Returns p. 280.

1 May 1784. Howell UNDERHILL and Nancy Gary, age 24, dau. of
John Gary. Sur. William Harrison. p. 35.

10 December 1810. Isham UNDERHILL and Lucy Richardson, dau.
Randolph and Annah Richardson. Married 13 December by Rev. Drewry
Lane. Sur. Seth Mason. p. 138.

3 October 1786. William UNDERHILL and Mary Anne Caroline Meacham,
dau. Anne Meacham. Married 7 October by Rev. John Cameron. Sur.
James Meacham. p. 43.

9 January 1796. Cain UNDERWOOD and Polly Harris. Sur. Timothy
Rose. p. 80.

3 November 1791. Edmund UNDERWOOD and Aggy Lynn. Sur. Weathers
Adams. Married by Rev. William Brown. p. 64.

26 December 1804. Claiborne UNDERWOOD and Sarah Long. Married
3 January 1805 by Rev. James Rogers. Sur. David Long. p. 116.

15 August 1796. Harbart UNDERWOOD and Nancy Moseley. Sur.
Robert Rose. p. 82.

27 November 1792. John UNDERWOOD and Rebecca Bush. Married 29
November by Rev. William Brown. Sur. Benjamin Hay. p. 69.

1 January 1803. Peterson UNDERWOOD and Eleanor Willis. Sur.
Zaccheus Ezell. p. 109.

7 November 1781. James VAUGHAN and Ann Moore, widow. James Vaughan of Greensville County. Married by Rev. John Meglamore. Sur. John Jones. p. 29.

12 June 1794. Joel VAUGHAN and Sally Pane. Married by Rev. William Brown. Ministers' Returns p. 269.

18 November 1802. Robert VAUGHAN and Lucy Harwell. Returned 16 December by Rev. Stith Parham. Sur. Archer Parker. Wit: John Hunt. p. 108.

5 June 1799. William VELVAIN and Patsy Stacy. Sur. Nicholas Stacy. p. 93.

28 October 1754. John VERELL and Susanna Moore. Sur. Edward Petway. p. 1.

17 November 1767. Aaron VINSON and Sarah Ogburn, dau. John Ogburn. Aaron Vinson of Carolina, son of John Vinson. Sur. John Ogburn, Jr. Wit: Howell Hite. p. 11.

15 August 1771. John WALKER and Hanna Hunt, widow. Sur. Augustine Claiborne. Wit: John Pennington and Robert Hankinson. p. 15.

13 May 1807. John M. WALKER and Mary R. Harrison. Sur. Pleasant Hunnicutt. p. 125.

18 February 1796. Robert WALKER and Mary Smith, dau. Patience Smith. Robert Walker of Dinwiddie County. Sur. Newitt Drew. Married by Rev. John Easter. p. 80.

25 November 1788. John WALL and Fanny Loftin, dau. Frederick Loftin. Married 17 December by Rev. John Meglamore. Sur. Henry Loftin. p. 52.

19 September 1804. Mial WALL and Sally D. Wallis, dau. Jesse Wallis. Married 20 September by Rev. Drewry Lane. Sur. William Judkins. p. 116.

2 June 1773. Michael WALL and Mary Harrison, widow of Henry Harrison. Sur. Chappell Gee. p. 17.

5 May 1798. Michael WALL and Elizabeth Mason, dau. Thomas Mason. Returned 17 May by Rev. Stith Parham. Sur. Benjamin Wyche. Wit: William Tomlinson, Jr. p. 90.

21 December 1802. Colston O. WALLIS and Polly Lamb, dau. John Lamb, deceased, ward of Nicholas Presson. Sur. Manson Wilson. Married 23 December by Rev. Drewry Lane. p. 109.

2 September 1808. Jesse WALLIS and Charlotte Faison. Married 8 September by Rev. Drewry Lane. Sur. Thomas Hunt. Wit: James Dillard. p. 129.

5 March 1771. Francis WARD and Sarah Webb, dau. Robert Webb. Francis Ward of North Carolina. Sur. Robert Land. Wit: Nathaniel Webb. p. 14.

21 April 1810. James WATKINS and Nancy D. White. Married 24 April by Rev. Drewry Lane. Sur. Jonathan Coker. p. 136.

2 November 1788. Joseph WATKINSON and Sally Porter. Married by Rev. John Meglamore. Ministers' Returns p. 261.

20 August 1787. Archabald WATLERS and Sarah Gibbons. Sur. Lawrence Gibbons. Wit: James Gibbons. p. 48.

7 March 1795. Robert WATSON and Rebecca Dunn, dau. Thomas Dunn. Sur. Thomas Johnson. p. 76.

4 July 1791. Benjamin WEATHERS and Temperance Johnson. Sur. John Johnson. Married by Rev. William Brown. p. 63.

1 January 1801. John T. WEATHERS and Nancy Hobbs. Sur. Jesse Wren. p. 100.

8 December 1801. Nathan WEATHERS and Nancy Zills, consent of Lucy Zills. Sur. Isaac Bendall. p. 104.

16 December 1786. Benjamin WEAVER and Fanny Andews, age 22, dau. of Ledeay Andrews. Sur. John Gary, Sr. Wit: John Gary, Jr., and Harris Cotton. Married by Rev. John Meglamore. p. 44.

24 July 1782. Henry WEAVER and Mary Jarratt. Sur. David Jones. p. 30.

15 April 1809. Anthony WEBB and Jincy Stephenson. Sur. John Stephenson. p. 132.

31 October 1801. William WEEKS and Mary Ann Lessenberry. Married 19 November by Rev. Augustine Heath. Sur. William Lessenberry. p. 103.

1 October 1807. William B. WELLONS and Sally Burt. Married 8 October by Rev. Drewry Lane. Sur. Herod Burt. p. 126.

17 January 1810. David WELLS and Elizabeth E. Wells. Sur. Baker Wells. p. 135.

6 December 1806. Joseph WELLS and Sally Porch. Married by Rev. James Gibbons. Ministers' Returns p. 284.

4 May 1804. William M. WELLS and Lucy Dunn. Sur. Nathaniel Raines. p. 114.

19 December 1797. John Jordan WEST and Polly Cooper, dau. James Cooper. Sur. Jordan Jones. Married 21 December by Rev. Drewry Lane. p. 88

2 February 1808. Benjamin H. WHITE and Sally Clark. Married 4 February by Rev. Drewry Lane. Sur. James Coker. p. 127.

17 May 1785. Charles WHITE and Rebekah Carrel, dau. William Carrel who is surety. Charles White of Surry County. p. 37.

4 April 1805. James WHITE, Jr. and Levina Bains. Married 11 April by Rev. Jesse Halleman, Sr. Sur. Elijah Bain. p. 117.

26 December 1789. Augustine WHITEHEAD and Lucy Knight, dau. Elizabeth Knight. Sur. Thomas Horn. p. 58.

29 December 1801. Edmund WHITEHEAD and Rebecca Spain. Sur. William Whitehead. p. 104. See Edwin Whitehead.

------ 1801. Edwin WHITEHEAD and Rebecca Spain. Married by Rev. Stith Parham. Minister's Returns p. 277. See Edmund Whitehead.

24 December 1807. Gray WHITEHEAD and Frankey Spain, consent of William and Mary Spain. Sur. Thomas Spain. p. 127.

7 January 1801. Mark WHITEHEAD and Nancy Spain. Sur. Richard Horn. Married by Rev. Stith Parham. p. 100.

27 January 1784. Mathew Cole WHITEHEAD and Lucrecia Cocke. Married by Rev. John Meglamore. Ministers' Returns p. 323.

3 January 1797. Matthew WHITEHEAD and Margaret Knight. Sur. Harmon Horn. p. 85. Double wedding: See Harmon Horn.

6 August 1791. Robert WHITEHEAD and Rebecca Spain. Sur. James Spain. Married by Rev. George Parham. p. 63.

18 December 1798. William WHITEHEAD and Catharine Horn. Sur. Richard Horn. p. 92.

15 September 1791. Edward WHITEHORN and Sally Clanton. Sur. Charles Champion. Married by Rev. William Brown. p. 63.

17 December 1810. George WHITEHORN and Jackey Clanton. Sur. Robert Clanton. p. 138.

17 October 1800. John WHITEHORN and Phoebe Felts. Sur. William Whitehorn. p. 98.

3 September 1801. Philemon WHITEHORN and Susanna Simmons. Sur. William Whitehorn. p. 102.

7 January 1790. Thomas WHITEHORN and Sally Felts. Married 21 January by Rev. John Mason. Sur. Abel Ezell. p. 59.

26 March 1803. William WHITEHORN and Zilpah Rose. Married 31
March by Rev. Stith Parham. Sur. William Jarrad. p. 110.

20 May 1803. William WHITEHORN, Sr. and Patsy Whittington, dau.
Howell Whittington. Sur. James Seaborn. p. 111.

18 August 1804. Harrison WHITFIELD and Polly Sledge, ward of
Mary Sledge. Married 29 August by Rev. James Rogers. Sur.
Benjamin Sturdivant. p. 115.

23 December 1801. Wilkins WHITFIELD and Polly Sturdivant. Sur.
Harrison Whitfield. p. 104.

19 July 1782. William WHITFIELD and Elizabeth Tomlinson. Married
26 July by Rev. Jesse Lee. Sur. Alexander Tomlinson. p. 30.

9 May 1796. Benjamin WILBORNE, Jr. and Rebecca Oliver. Sur.
William Malone, Jr. Married by Rev. Stith Parham. p. 82.

4 December 1806. Harris WILBORNE and Polly Berryman. Married
24 December by Rev. James Rogers. Sur. Benjamin Harrison. p. 122.

4 June 1801. James WILBORNE and Milcah Cain. Sur. George Randolph.
Married by Rev. Stith Parham. p. 101.

15 September 1810. James WILBORNE and Nancy Wilborne. Sur.
Harrison Wynne. p. 136.

9 April 1792. John WILBORNE, Jr. and Lucy Mabry. Married 12
April by Rev. William Brown. Sur. Abel Mabry. p. 67.

24 April 1798. William WILBORNE and Rebecca Wilborne. Married
26 April by Rev. Henry Moss. Sur. Gabriel Moss. p. 89.

2 August 1792. Burwell WILKERSON and Priscilla Mitchell. Sur.
Reaps. Mitchell. Married by Rev. Henry Moss. p. 67.

1 September 1791. Henry WILKERSON and Susanna Anderson. Married
8 September by Rev. Henry Moss. Sur. McDuel Anderson. p. 63.

1 February 1786. James WILKERSON and Nancy Morris, dau. John
Morris. Sur. Abraham Hatton. Wit: William Milner. Married 25
February by Rev. Jesse Lee. p. 41.

16 August 1781. Joel WILKERSON and Ann Vaughan, dau. Thomas
Vaughan. Joel Wilkerson of Greensville County. Sur. Thomas
Hunt. Wit: Evans Mabry and Barnard Wilkerson. p. 28.

30 March 1803. Joel WILKERSON and Nancy McKinney, dau. Rebecca
McKinney. Sur. William Wilkerson. p. 110.

26 December 1789. John WILKERSON and Rockey Scoggon. Married 29 December by Rev. Henry Moss. Sur. William Sykes. p. 58.

4 July 1799. Richard WILKERSON and Nancy Hutchings. Returned 1 August by Rev. Augustine Heath. p. 93.

1 December 1796. William WILKERSON and Polly Hutchings, dau. John Hutchings. Married 22 December by Rev. Henry Moss. Sur. Henry Rives. p. 84.

30 September 1796. Ambrose WILKINS and Patsey Blunt, ward of Peter Jones. Sur. James Boisseau. p. 83.

14 May 1800. John Douglas WILKINS and Agnes Wyatt, ward of John Trizevant. Sur. John Wyatt. p. 97.

21 December 1795. Samuel WILLCOX and Nancy Parsons, dau. Henry Parsons. Married 24 December by Rev. Drewry Lane. p. 79.

17 February 1780. Charles WILLIAMS and Susanna Jarrard, dau. Nicholas Jarrard who is surety. p. 25.

29 April 1788. Charles WILLIAMS and Nancy Flowers. Married 2 May by Rev. John Meglamore. Sur. Philip Williams. Wit: Robert and Sarah Andrews. p. 51.

12 December 1787. David WILLIAMS and Mary Peebels, consent of John Potts. Sur. William Sykes. p. 49.

18 December 1797. John WILLIAMS and Polly Harrup, dau. Anna Harrup. Sur. Isaac Bendall. p. 87.

16 November 1789. Philip WILLIAMS and Phebe Loftin. Married 19 November by Rev. John Meglamore. Sur. John Williams. Wit: William Loftin. p. 57.

30 June 1806. Reuben WILLIAMS and Jane Tucker. Married by Rev. James Gibbons. Ministers' Returns p. 284.

6 December 1785. William WILLIAMS and Elizabeth Webb. Sur. Charles Judkins. p. 40.

13 January 1790. Henry WILLIAMSON and Rebecca Mason. Married 16 January by Rev. John Paup. Sur. David Mason. p. 59.

15 December 1792. Jesse WILLIAMSON and Elizabeth Marable. Married 22 December by Rev. William Brown. Sur. Edward Pennington. p. 69.

16 January 1783. John WILLIAMSON and Martha Gilliam. Sur. Jesse Williamson. p. 32.

29 February 1808. Joseph WILLIAMSON and Hannah Mason. Married
1 March by Rev. James Rogers. Sur. James Dillard.   p. 128.

29 June 1803. Matthew WILLIAMSON and Polly Lanier, consent of
Buckner Lanier. Married 30 June by Rev. James Rogers. Sur. Cyrill
Avery, Jr.   p. 111.

10 December 1787. Person WILLIAMSON and Mary Mason, dau. David
Mason. Sur. Nathaniel Clanton.   p. 48.

17 September 1785. Thomas WILLIAMSON and Martha Graves, dau.
Solomon Graves, deceased, and ward of William Graves. Thomas
Williamson son of Arthur Williamson, deceased, and ward of Jesse
Williamson. Sur. Frederick Pennington. Wit: Ann Pennington,
Mary Pennington, Nathaniel Clanton and Marcus Pennington.   p. 39.

28 July 1810. Willis WILLIAMSON and Nancy B. Cornwell. Married
9 August by Rev. Drewry Lane. Sur. Samuel B. Cornwell.   p. 136.

3 January 1807. Manson WILSON and Frances G. Parham. Sur. John
Andrews.   p. 123.

18 August 1785. Mathew WINEY and Sarah Biggins. Married by
Rev. John Meglamore. Ministers' Returns p. 258.

18 February 1790. Curtis WINFIELD and Polly Cain. Sur. Robert
Parham.   p. 59.

31 October 1792. Ephraim WINFIELD and Nancy Tucker. Sur. Thomas
Eppes. Married by Rev. George Parham.   p. 68.

6 January 1783. William WINFIELD, Jr. and Elizabeth Tucker,
ward of David Thweatt. Sur. Peter Cain. Wit: William Cain and
Isham Smith.   p. 32.   See William Wingfield.

1 February 1798. William WINFIELD and Mary Tucker, dau. Robert
Rucker, deceased, consent of Stith Parham. Sur. Thomas Eppes.
Married by Rev. Stith Parham.   p. 89.

6 January 1783. William WINGFIELD, Jr. and Elizabeth Rucker,
ward of David Thweatt. Sur. Peter Cain. Wit: William Cain and
Isham Smith.   p. 32.   See William Winfield.

17 March 1791. John WINN and Caty Stokes. Married by Rev. Henry
Moss. Ministers' Returns p. 264.

18 December 1790. Edmund WOOD and Elizabeth Jones. Sur. Moses
Booth.   p. 62.

29 December 1786. William WOODLAND and Mary Hewitt. Married 2
January 1787 by Rev. John Meglamore. Sur. Isaac Collier.   p. 45.

13 December 1793. Francis WOOLFOLD and Eliza Taylor. Sur. Benjamin B. Rosser. p. 72.

26 January 1805. Dyson WOOTON and Nancy Calthorp, consent of Edward Wootten for Dyson. Married 29 January by Rev. Drewry Lane. Sur. Benjamin Hargrave. p. 117.

19 November 1802. Jack WOOTON and Mason Blizzard. Married 25 November by Rev. Drewry Lane. Sur. Abraham James. p. 108.

20 April 1801. Maclin WOOTON and Thamer Freeman. Sur. Charles Roberts. p. 101.

29 October 1789. Edward WOOTTON, Jr. and Abigail Bailey, consent of Milley Sears. Sur. John Bains. p. 57.

3 November 1802. Edward WOOTTON and Martha Atkinson. Married 10 November by Rev. Drewry Lane. Sur. Jesse Bryant. Wit: Nicholas Johnson. p. 108.

1 October 1785. Thomas WOOTTON and Mary Tomlinson, orphan, ward of William Tomlinson. Sur. Miles Birdsong. Wit: Joseph Birdsong and John Tomlinson. p. 39.

31 May 1800. William WOOTTON and Hannah Presson. Married 3 June by Rev. Drewry Lane. Sur. Thomas L. Presson. p. 97.

6 March 1804. James WOTTON and Miney Calthorp. Ma-rried 7 March by Rev. Drewry Lane who says Mimy (Jemima?). Sur. Thomas Edwards. p. 114.

17 December 1792. Bates WRENN and Clarissa Wrenn (Clarissa Jones). Sur. Anthony Sturdivant. Wit: Faith King. p. 69.

27 October 1810. James O. WRENN and Elizabeth Jarratt. Sur. Henry Wilkerson. Married by Rev. Drewry Lane. p. 137.

17 December 1785. Jesse WRENN and Mary Hall, dau. James Hall. Married 22 December by Rev. John Cameron. Sur. William Burge. Wit: William Bobbitt and John Tyus. p. 41. Double wedding: see William Burge.

27 December 1797. John WRENN and Frances Oliver. Married 7 January 1798 by Rev. Stith Parham. Sur. Lowell H. Walker. Wit: William Fowler. p. 88.

23 August 1790. Richard WRENN and Sarah (Charity) Smith. Sur. Nicholas Presson. p. 61.

30 December 1797. Richard WRENN and Rebecca Smith. Married 2 January 1798 by Rev. Drewry Lane. Sur. William Cross. p. 88.

5 March 1801. Thomas WRENN and Rebecca Gilliam. Sur. Carter Gilliam. p. 100.

31 July 1787. James WRIGHT and Katey Glover. Sur. Joseph Glover. p. 47.

20 March 1788. John WRIGHT and Livina Tuder, dau. Henry Tuder. Sur. Howell McLemore. Wit: David Mason. p. 50.

21 November 1798. Reuben WRIGHT and Anna Gilbert. Sur. Gray Barker. p. 91.

23 July 1806. Willis WRIGHT and Mary Long. Married 24 July by Rev. James Rogers. Sur. Charles Long. p. 121.

20 May 1758. Benjamin WYCHE and Elizabeth Peete, dau. Samuel Peete who consents. Sur. Thomas Peters. p. 4.

18 July 1788. Benjamin WYCHE and Elizabeth Mason. Sur. John Mason. p. 51.

15 October 1761. George WYCHE and Mary -----. Sur. Nathaniel Dobie. p. 6.

22 November 1807. Benjamin WYNNE and Sally D. Wall. Married 26 November by Rev. James Rogers. Sur. Jesse Wallis. p. 126.

3 February 1785. Buckner WYNNE and Frances Wynn. Married by Rev. John Meglamore. Ministers' Returns p. 323.

3 March 1803. Ephraim WYNNE and Nancy Stokes. Married 8 March by Rev. Stith Parham. Sur. John Lilly, Jr. p. 110.

6 January 1807. Ephraim WYNNE and Fereby Owen. Married 22 January by Rev. James Rogers. Sur. William H. Niblett. p. 123.

19 November 1792. Gray WYNNE and Edith Sturdivant. Sur. Robert Sturdivant. Married by Rev. George Parham. p. 69.

16 December 1785. Green WYNNE and Hanna Tyus, dau. Lewis Tyus. Green son of John Wynne. Sur. William Wynne. Wit: Charles Sturdivant, Mathew Sturdivant and Lucy Wynne. p. 40.

27 February 1799. Harrison WYNNE and Sally Bonds. Sur. Philip Bailey. p. 93.

2 October 1800. John WYNNE and Susanna Wynne. Sur. Peterson Wynne. Married by Rev. Stith Parham. p. 98.

7 November 1785. Joshua WYNNE, Jr. and Sarah Wynne, dau. Mathew Wynne. Sur. John Sturdivant. Wit: Buckner Winn. Married 27 November by Rev. Jesse Lee. p. 40.

11 August 1798. Joshua WYNNE and Nancy Wynne. Sur. Robert Wynne. p. 91.

13 January 1778. Matthew WYNNE, Jr. and Anne Lilly. Matthew son of William Wynn. Sur. Stith Wynn. Wit: Hartwell Marable and Frederick Lilly. p. 23.

16 August 1785. Matthew WYNNE, Sr. and Sarah Biggins, (widow). Sur. James Glover, Sr. Married 18 August by Rev. John Meglamore. p. 38.

28 October 1788. Matthew WYNNE and Winny Lilly Married 30 October by Rev. John Meglamore. Sur. William Wynne. p. 52.

26 March 1796. Peter WYNNE and Elizabeth Wynne. Married 31 March by Rev. Henry Moss. Sur. William Wynne. p. 81.

7 May 1800. Peterson WYNNE and Dolly Sturdivant. Sur. William Whitfield. p. 97.

23 May 1798. Robert WYNNE and Betsy Sledge. Sur. Robert Sturdivant. Returned 18 July by Rev. Henry Moss. p. 90.

10 March 1798. William WYNNE and Polly Parham, dau. Abraham Parham. Sur. Thomas Parham. p. 89.

19 September 1785. William YATES and Elizabeth Booth, dau. George Booth who is surety. William Yates of Amelia County. Wit: Thomas Lundie. p. 39.

26 September 1766. Thomas YOUNG and Katherine Barlow, widow. Sur. David Mason. Wit: James Mason and James Jones. p. 10.

19 July 1792. Jesse ZILLS and Elizabeth Bendall. Married 29 July by Rev. Henry Moss. Sur. Euclid Langford. p. 67.

4 February Marcus ZILLS and Mary Zills. Sur. John Lilly. p. 59.

29 May 1810. Peebles ZILLS and Elizabeth Pennington, dau. Nancy Pennington. Sur. Benjamin W. Carlos. p. 136.

Mary	89

A.

Abernathy
Mary	69

Adams
Celia	37
Crecy	80
Lucy	37
Mary P.	52
Nancy	34
Polly	30,38
Priscilla	67
Sarah	9,31

Adkins
Elizabeth	33
Mary	64
Polly Simmons	78
Sally	76
Sarah	53

Ambros
Lilly	20

Ambrose
Elizabeth	75

Ambruss
Elizabeth	75

Anderson
Sarah	40
Susanna	85

Anderton
Polly	45

Andrews
Abbey	29
Anna	49
Dorothy	72
Elizabeth	14,51,58
Fanny	83
Fathy	66
Joanne	6
Lucy	4
Nancy	6
Polly	28,35
Polly B.	56
Sally	21,24,47
Susanna	47

Andriton
Polly	45

Armstrong
Elizabeth	47

Atkins
Winifred	77

Atkinson
Agath	14
Jemima	67
Martha	88
Susanna	43

Atkison
Winny	52

Avent
Aney	53
Angelila	44
Molly	22
Polly	19
Rebecca	32
Ruinah	18

Avery
Elizabeth	32
Martha	7
Sally	48
Sarah	14

B

Bailey
Abigail	88
Edna	67
Lucy	64
Nancy	31
Polly	3,43
Rebecca	4
Willy	21

Bains-Baines
Anne	71
Creacy	42
Lavina	84
Mary	42
Sarah	12

Baird
Ann	57
Mary	33

Banns
Mary	42

Barham
Elizabeth	29
Milley	40
Patty	50
Polly	57

Barker
Catherine	70
Celia	10
Elizabeth 3,19,(2),71	
Lucy	10,48
Molly	51
Nancy	6,24
Polly	26

Barlor
Nancy	46

Barlow
Katherine	90

Barnes
Elizabeth	44

Barrow
Nancy	50

Bass
Elizabeth	12

Battle
Agnes	42

Batts
Martha	(2), 69

Baylis
Mary	39

Beard
Rebecca	79

Beddingfield
Isabella	48

Bell
Elizabeth	34
Mildred Lucas	54
Nancy	80
Polly	59
Rebeckah	66
Sally Wilks	58

Belsches
Margaret	14
Sarah	74

Bendall
Elizabeth	90
Judah	2
Judy	2
Sarah	74

Berriman-Berryman
Polly	85
Rebecca	61

Betts
Anne	28
Frances	81
Rebecca	43

Biggins
Fanny	65
Molly	7
Sarah	87.90

Binns
Elizabeth	44
Martha	70

Birdsong
Patsy	12
Polly	19
Rebecca	8 ,9
Sally	66

Birt
Elizabeth	58

Bishop
Elizabeth	52
Keziah	24
Lydia	56
Sally	59
Silvia	49

Blizzard
  Mason 88
  Milly 23

Blow
  Betsy 11
  Mary 4
  Nancy 73
  Rebecca 20
  Sally 4

Blunt
  Ann 30
  Dolly 30
  Patsey 86

Bobbitt
  Betsy 68
  Elizabeth 68
  Polly 22

Bonds
  Sally 89
  Susan 72

Bonner
  Jane 32
  Margaret 7
  Patsy 16

Booth
  Celia 60
  Eliza 38
  Elizabeth 44 ,90
  Mary 36
  Nancy 5
  Patsey 66
  Polly 32

Bottom
  Martha 73
  Rebecca 60

Bowles
  Nancy 44

Bracy
  Elizabeth 8

Bradley
  Sarah 52

Brantley
  Elizabeth 3

Bridges
  Elizabeth 31

Briggs
  Agness 46
  Elizabeth 45,64
  Frances 9,70
  Jane 74
  Mary 8,10,61,75
  Nancy 54
  Rebecca 40
  Sarah 22
  Susanna 58

Broadnax
  Mary 30

Brock
  Rhoda 5

Brockwell
  Beea 22

Brown-Browne
  A-ba 55
  Hannah 38
  Polly 41

Brunt
  Priscilla 68

Bryan
  Peggy 41

Bryant
  Nancy 42

Bullock
  Priscilla 54

Burges
  Christian 80

Burk
  Nancy 61

Burt
  Sally 83

Burrow
  Mary± 53

Bush
  Rebecca 81

Butler
  Anne 47
  Mary 14
  Sally Walter 14,45

Byrd
  Polly 8

C

Cain
  Creasy 20
  Elizabeth 1,26
  Frances 71
  Martha 2
  Milcah 85
  Polly 87

Calthorp
  Mimy 88
  Miney 88
  Nancy 88

Cannady
  Mary 17
  Silvey 21

Capps
  Susanna 17

Cargill
  Elizabeth 43

Carlos
  Mary 21

Carrel-Carrell
  Edy 24
  Nancy 67
  Patience 58
  Patty 3
  Polly 66
  Rebekah 84
  Susanna 28

Carrol
  Rachel 75

Carter
  Dolly 43
  Lucy 72
  Lucy Wright 52
  Rebecca 4

Chambliss
  Betsy 31
  Elizabeth 15
  Frances M. 30
  Judah 42
  Martha 51,74
  Mary 30,60
  Polly 30
  Sally 47

Champion
  Keziah 49
  Rebecca 34

Chappell
  Ann 60
  Creesy 14
  Elizabeth 5,61,67
  Elizabeth E. 36
  Elizabeth Mason 11
  Lidda 55
  Lucretia Tucker 68
  Martha 2,46
  Mary 51
  Pamelia 16
  Phebe 68
  Polly 21
  Rebecca 50
  Sally 14
  Sarah B. 30
  Susanna 25

Cheesman
  Mildred 58
  Polly 19

Claiborne
  Ann 18
  Elizabeth 64
  Lucy Herbert 18
  Susanna 44

Clanton
Jackey	84
Mildred	62
Rebecca	4
Sally	84

Clark-Clarke
Elizabeth	37
Sally	84
Sarah	28

Clary
Jincy	56
Nancy	47
Susanna	65

Clements
Amey	40
Lucy	73

Cleveland
Martha	7
Patsey	7

Cocke
Lucy Herbert	79
Lucrecia	84
Mary	39
Polly	10

Cocks
Sally	77

Coggin
Elizabeth	21

Coker
Dilley	18
Martha	13
Peggy	20

Cole
Elizabeth	18,38
Polly	23
Sally W.	31

Collier
Nancy	36
Rebeccah	69

Comar
Mary	62

Cook-Cooke
Betsy	74
Mary	11,39
Polly	7
Sarah	45,54

Cooper
Charlotte	55
Lucrecy	74
Lucy	76
Mary	46
Nancy	51
Polly	31,79,83

Cornet
Martha	52

Cornwell
Nancy B.	87
Polly	38

Cotton
Celia	73
Deidama	19
Drucilla	5
Elizabeth	19
Polly C.	7
Rebecca	52
Susannah	5
Sylvia	75

Creagh
Peggy	21

Cross
Lucy	62
Mary	36
Patsy	3
Rebecca	12
Susanna	40

Cureton
Betsey	22

Curtis
Sixty	48

Cypress
Sacky	44

D

Dancy
Elizabeth	75

Davis
Elizabeth	72
Lucretia	27
Lucy	10,15.45
Rebecca	50
Selah	25
Viney	71
Viny	67

Davison
Fanny	45
Lucy	62

Debbericks
Nancy	16

Dobie
Claramond	16

Downman
Agnes Archer	9

Driver
Judith	12

Dunn
Elizabeth	12,35
Jane	61
Lucy	83
Mary	43,48,57
Rebecca	83
Ruth	61
Susan	73

E

Echols
Nancy	65

Eckels-Eckles-Eckols
Hannah	61
Martha	80
Sally	41
Susanna	45

Eggleston
Patty	11

Edmunds
Charlotte	9
Elizabeth	36
Mary	16
Sarah	23
Susanna	23
Tempy	75

Edwards
Mary	5
Rebecca	6
Rosy	17
Sarah	20

Eldridge
Ann	14,70
Elizabeth	53,70
Nancy	70
Sarah	70

Ellis
Anne	17
Catharine	16
Elizabeth	3
Frances	32
Lucy	6
Martha	24
Mary	24,25,67
Nancy	32
Polly	66
Rebecca	41
Sally	32
Susanna	3

Eppes
Martha	32
Susanna	33

Evans
Hannah	56
Polly	(2),61
Sally	1

Ezell
Lucy	42
Nancy	52
Patsey	43
Phebe	3

F

Fagan
Ruana 63

Faison
  Charlotte 82
  Polly 11

Felts
  Angelila 49
  Betsey 72
  Eliza 31
  Elizabeth 72
  Mary 25
  Patty 40
  Phoebe 84
  Polly 33
  Sally 20,28,84
  Silvyer 74

Fiers
  Sarah 53

Figures
  Mary 47

Fisher
  Elizabeth 57
  Polly 63

Flowers
  Elizabeth 55
  Nancy 86
  Selah 48

Fogg
  Elizabeth 75
  Judith 39

Fort
  Elizabeth 57
  Mason 67

Fowler
  Mary B. 27
  Sarah 16

Freeman
  Angelila 49
  Anna 27
  Elizabeth 32,42
  Keziah 55
  Mary 27
  Patsey 26
  Sally 11
  Seesela 6
  Thamer 88

G

Garland
  Mary 38

Garrettson
  Sally Hanson 75

Gary
  Nancy 81
  Sally U. 70

Gay
  Mary 11

Gee
  Amy 78
  Boyce 27
  Boys 66
  Elizabeth 53
  Jane 35
  Mary 33
  Patsy 52
  Rebecca 79

Gibbons
  Elizabeth 20,35
  Mary 74
  Polly 61
  Sarah 83

Gilbert
  Anna 89
  Edith 55
  Elizabeth 6
  Mary 23
  Sally 20

Gilliam
  Ann 44
  Dorothea 63
  Elizabeth 19,50
  Lucy 51
  Lurana 44
  Martha 8.86
  Martha J. 13
  Mary 9,31,53
  Phebe 10
  Polly W. 69
  Priscilla 45
  Rebecca 88
  Sally 42
  Sarah 11,19
  Winnifred 18

Glover
  Katey 89
  Mary 50
  Nancy 36,37
  Rebecca 37

Goodwyn
  Martha 70
  Nancy 75
  Sally 46

Graves
  Ann 64,68
  Elizabeth 71
  Lucy 66
  Martha 87
  Polly 26
  Rebecca 2,15
  Sally 15,64

Gray
  Amelia 58

Green
  Elizabeth 43
  Martha 7
  Mary 15
  Nancy 11
  Rebecca 51
  Sarah 60

Griffin
  Elizabeth 45
  Mary 60

Grizzard
  Lucy 3
  Mary 5
  Nancy 53
  Polly 57

H

Haile
  Susanna 56

Hails
  Elizabeth 1

Halcome
  Martha 69

Hall
  Elizabeth 23,62
  Martha C. 34
  Mary 88
  Nancy 81
  Rebecca 12
  Sally 10

Hancock
  Elizabeth 28
  Jane 65
  Mary 5,63
  Nancy 18

Hargrave
  Cherry 8
  Elizabeth 40
  Lettuce 28
  Lucy 80
  Sally 26
  Willy 45

Harper
  Ann 1,73

Hart
  Charity 34
  Cherry 34
  Jenny 27

Harris
  Catharine 41
  Lucy 56
  Polly 81

Harrison
  Ann Carter 17
  Harriot 63
  Jackey 80
  Mary 59,82
  Mary E. 14
  Mary R. 82
  Mary S. 39
  Nancy 19,43
  Rebecca 76
  Susan 48

Harrup
  Polly 86

Hartley
Clarissa 38
Drada 21
Elizabeth 30
Molly 29
Polly 29

Harvill
Luraney 54

Harwell
Lucy 82

Harwood
Ann Bell 65
Fanny M. 38
Levina 64
Nancy 69
Nancy Murray 21
Polly 26,57
Rebecca 56

Hawthorne
Betsey 34
Elizabeth 46
Lucy 52
Rebecca 13
Susanna 55

Hay
Margaret 33,34
Molly 3

Hays
Ruth 65

Hearn
Catharine 63
Rebecca 17
Sally 73

Heath
Elizabeth 2,75
Jane 23
Jemima 70
Sally 57
Tabitha 80

Hern
Polly 72

Heron
Mary 42

Hewitt
Martha 56
Mary 87
Lucy 19
Lucy G. 4

Hicks
Mary 58,79
Rhoda 11
Sally 5
Sarah 43

Hines
Elizabeth 54
Mary 16

Hines (Cont'd)
Nancy 41
Nanny 21
Sally 16

Hinton
Sally Jones 46

Hill
Ann 3
Caty 19
Hannah 60
Rebecca 39,49
Sarah 72
Susannah 39

Hite
Rhody 36

Hix
Cherry 25
Mary 79
Nancy 43
Patsy 14

Hobbs
Drusilla 77
Edy 69
Frances 32
Lizza 79
Lucy 17
Mary 4,34
Nancy 34,79,83
Permely 26
Sally 48
Sarah 22
Selah 77
Susanna 37

Hogwood
Polly 69

Holdsworth
Ann 32

Holloman
Sarah 31

Holloway
Cherry 25
Lilley 44
Rhoda 4

Holt
Amey Wyche 54
Betsy 3,38
Jincy 18
Lucy 17
Nancy 18,54
Temperance 57

Hood
Charlotte 46
Polly 2

Horn
Catharine 84
Elizabeth 79
Peggy 76
Sally 66

Howard
Betsey 35

Hubbard
Silvia 22

Hudson
Elizabeth Arnold 73
Janey 13

Hunnicutt
Mary 10

Hunt
Athaliah 80
Betty 17
Elizabeth 45
Hannah 82
Lucy 34
Nancy 36
Patsy 28
Susanna 62

Huson
Mary 75

Hutchings
Caty 40
Lucy 54
Nancy 86
Polly 86

I

Irby
Ann 18

Isel
Polly 57

Ivey
Eady 40
Mariah 5
Mary 41
Polly 41

J

Jackson
Catharine 41
Frances 32
Rebecca 1

Jarrad
Charity 36
Elizabeth 8,45
Nancy 7
Rebecca 8
Sally P. 57

Jarrard
Susanna 86

Jarrat-Jarratt
Elizabeth 41,88
Mary 57,83
Nancy 59
Rebekah 71
Sarah 63

Jefferson
  Amey   23

Jenkins
  Mary   33

Jennett
  Mary   34
  Rebecca   49

Jennings
  Ann   71

Johnson
  Betsy   26
  Elizabeth   68
  Mary   7
  Phebe   10
  Polly   80
  Rebecca   43,78
  Sarah   2,17
  Sillar   43
  Temperance   83

Jones
  Ann   61
  Ann Barber   55
  Catharine   71
  Charlotte   25
  Clarissa   69,88
  Elizabeth   42,44,87
  Jane   39
  Larana   15
  Lucretia   74
  Lucy   23,28,46 ,53
  Martha   18
  Mary9,10,(2)26,31,46,78
  Nancy   78
  Patty   14
  Priscilla   55
  Rebecca   44,50
  Sally   63
  Susan   16
  Susanna   8,68

Jordan
  Lucy   65
  Nancy   51
  Polly   12

Judkins
  Amelia   66
  Ann   27
  Frances   37
  Lucy   56
  Ruiana   25
  Sally   64
  Susanna   38

K

Kelley
  Anney   4
  Mary   62
  Sally   78

Kenibrugh
  Nancy   38

Kenniburgh
  Sally   16

King
  Elizabeth   63
  Martha Hall   77
  Nancy   60
  Sarah   59

Kitchen
  Avarilla   81
  Lucy   58

Knight
  Elizabeth   78
  Lucy   84
  Margaret   84
  Martha   77
  Mary   41
  Prudence   39
  Sally   79
  Temperance   51

L

Lamb
  Elizabeth   19
  Mary   7
  Polly   82
  Sally   17

Lancaster
  Zilla   60

Land
  Agnes   37
  Elizabeth   37
  Jincy   8
  Jiney H.   8
  Jiny   56
  Mary   58
  Patsey   66
  Rebecca   16
  Ruth   50

Lain-Lane-Layne
  Mary H.   71
  Nancy   3
  Rebecca   (2),4
  Sally   4,5

Lanier
  Patsey   52
  Polly   87
  Susanna   2

Lashby
  Sally   17

Lashley
  Sally   17

Leath
  Elizabeth   59
  Lydia   16

Lee
  Celia   61
  Elizabeth   48
  Martha   13
  Mary   35

Lessenberry
  Mary Ann   83

Lewis
  Jincy   14
  Polly   60

Lilley-Lilly
  Anne   90
  Lucy   8
  Winny   90

Linn
  Clary   39

Little
  Nancy   16

Lloyd
  Ann   35

Loftin
  Elizabeth   7
  Fanny   82
  Lucy   28
  Nancy   45,63
  Patsy   3
  Peggy   64
  Phebe   86
  Polly   64
  Sally   38
  Susanna   62

Long
  Agnes   17
  Anna   6
  Mary   89
  Nancy   65
  Rebecca   50
  Sarah   81

Longbottom
  Mary   50

Lounsford
  Susanna   51

Lucas
  Rebecca   27
  Susanns   2

Lynn
  Aggy   81

M

Mabry
  Lucy   85
  Olive   1
  Phoebe   1

Magee
  Elizabeth   28,42
  Judith   50
  Lucy   51
  Mary   25,50
  Nancy   10
  Rebecca   25
  Sally   51

Malone
  Amey 71
  Elizabeth 10,16
  Frances 42
  Lucy 27
  Mary 13,59
  Rebecca 59
  Sally 81

Mangam
  Lucy 8

Mangum
  Jemima 52
  Mary 52
  Sarah 69

Mannery
  Nancy 72

Maning
  Mary 28

Manny
  Mary 28

Manry
  Silviah 6

Marable
  Elizabeth 86

Marks
  Susanna J. 75

Mason
  Ann 47
  Elizabeth52(2)70,82,89
  Hannah 87
  Lucrecia 53
  Lucy 7
  Lucy M. 21
  Mary 6,10,(2)76,78,87
  Nancy 7
  Patsy 67
  Polly 57
  Rebecca 70,86
  Sally 34
  Susanna 29

Massenburg
  Barbara 61
  Elizabeth 59
  Lucy 55
  Mary E. 9
  Susanna H. 23

Mayo
  Polly 68

Mays
  Polly 71

Meacham-Meachum
  Diana 69
  Dyaney 69
  Lilley 54
  Lucy 24
  Mary Ann Carolina 81

Meacham-Meachum (cont'd)
  Rebecca 50

Meglamore
  Betsy 4

Miller
  Mary Ann 28

Mitchell
  Amy 68
  Elizabeth 15
  Frances 9,10
  Franky 65
  Martha 80
  Mary 78
  Priscilla 59,85
  Scota 63
  Tabitha 6

Montgomery
  Sarah 56

Moody
  Betsy 72
  Elizabeth 61

Moore
  Ann 82
  Elizabeth 30
  Polly 44
  Sarah 15
  Susanna 38,82

Morgan
  Elizabeth 73
  Sarah 73

Morris-Morriss
  Aggy 5
  Nancy 85

Mosby
  Feraby 39

Mosley
  Fanny 73
  Nancy 81
  Pherabe 39
  Sally 55

Moss
  Edith 40
  Elizabeth 41,42
  Lucy 47
  Martha 43
  Peggy 33
  Polly 34
  Susanna 28,49

Moyler
  Judith Q. 51

Munds
  Betsy 74
  Sally 13

Murdock
  Sally 20

Murphey
  Jincey 5

Murrell
  Lucy 5

Myrick
  Fanny 59
  Lucy 59

Mc

McCormick
  Elizabeth 78

McCullock
  Penelope 65

McKinney
  Nancy 55

N

Neblett
  Sally 79

Neves
  Mary M. 53

Newby
  Mary 77

Newsom-Newsome
  Fanny 65
  Martha 70
  Nancy S. 50

Newsum
  Sally 38

Niblett
  Dolly 21
  Polly 81

Nicholson
  Anne 9,71
  Elizabeth 45
  Jane 47
  Mary 8,20,22
  Polly 11
  Rachel 77
  Sarah 11
  Susanna 35

Norris
  Mary 13
  Susanna 37

Northcross
  Polly 48

Norton
  Polly 9

O

Ogburn
Sarah 82

Oliver
Elizabeth 55
Frances 88
Jane 59
Lucy 75
Nancy 15
Rebecca 85
Sally 26
Susanna 2

O'Riley
Martha 35

Owen
Anne 26,53
Elizabeth 31
Fereby 89
Gincy 20
Lucy 30
Mary 12
Nancy 53
Polly 6
Sally 36
Susanna 21

P

Pair
Nancy 66
Winny 65

Pane
Sally 82

Parham
Amey 36
Anna 44
Elisha 69
Elizabeth 6,66
Elizabeth McLin 12
Frances 27,68
Frances G. 87
Frances Haddon 31
Jane 79
Lucretia 21,46,61
Martha 68
Mary 11,79
Mary Ann 80
Molly 61
Nancy 60,76
Polly 90
Rebecca 22,61
Sally 15
Sarah 29
Susan 56
Susanna 36
Susanna Kelly 60

Parker
Jane 11
Judah 36
Lucy 64
Martha 74
Mary 65
Mary Blunt 13
Rebecca 18
Sally 8
Sarah 62
Temperance 23

Parsons
Mary G. 75
Nancy 86

Partain
Rebecca 77

Partridge
Ann M. 75

Pate
Catherine 79
Lucy 31
Mary 1
Rebecca 63
Susanna 40,41

Peebles
Mary 86
Polly 53
Susanna 27

Peete
Elizabeth 9,89
Martha 9

Pennington
Elizabeth 24,54,63,90
Mary 80
Patsy 52
Polly 30
Sally 52
Sarah 56
Ursula 15

Pepper
Rebecca 31

Perkins
Polly 73

Peters
Elizabeth 53
Mary 62
Temperance 22

Pettway
Ann 2
Celia 48
Elizabeth 50
Phoebe 65
Rhoda 40
Sally 37
Susanna 65

Phillips
Rebecca 31

Phipps
Martha 67

Place
Lucy 6

Pleasants
Dolly 65
Mary 42
Sally 3

Porch
Elizabeth 48
Patsy 32
Rebecca 25
Sally 15,83

Porter
Sally 83

Powell
Elizabeth 7,13
Martha 22
Rebekah 31

Presson
Hannah 88
Jenney 18
Polly 32

Pride
Lucy 77

Prince 23,63

R

Raines
Betsy 81
Susanna 46,47

Rainey
Celia 22
Polly J. 46
Sally 71

Raley
Martha 35

Randolph
Elizabeth M. 24

Rawlings
Nancy 8
Rebecca 75

Ray
Frances 33
Sally 79

Redding
Elizabeth 33
Sarah 15
Susan 5
Susanna 29

Richardson
Lucy 81
Martha 12
Patty 27
Peggy 2
Viney 37

Rives
Charlotte 60
Elizabeth 16
Judith 9
Mary 63
Susanna 54

Rives (cont'd)
Selah 35
Winifred 59

Robarts-Roberts
Mary 47
Mary Seymour Degleish 8
Susanna B. 29

Robertson
Elizabeth J. 19
Jane 29
Mary Lucas 66
Nancy 1
Rhoda 55

Robinson
Rebecca 77

Rochell
Phebe 76
Sally 6
Selah 34
Susan 22

Roe
Elizabeth 26
Rebecca 76
Sally 25

Rogers-Rodgers
Anna 28
Anne 42
Milly 51
Suffiah 67

Roland
Elizabeth 72

Rollings
Amey 22
Elizabeth 35,43
Fanny 35

Rose
Elizabeth 45
Elizabeth Groves 43
Mary 70
Phebe 25
Rebecca 12
Sally 7
Zilpah 85

Rowland
Elizabeth 48,72

Ruffin
Jane Bland 18

S

Sammons
Betty 29
Cinthia 74
Hannah 6
Mary 34
Rebecca 57
Winny 80

Sanders
Jinsey 22

Sands
Dolly 73

Saunders
Amery 24
Amy 24
Patty 19

Scoggin-Scoggon
Elizabeth 20
Rockey 86

Scott
Elizabeth 14
Judah 60

Seaborne
Louisa 35

Sears
Milly 20

Seat
Lucy 72,73
Milley 49

Seward
Nancy 54

Shands
Frances 3
Phebe 74

Sharp
Cherry 24
Elizabeth 24

Sikes
Ann 23

Sills
Ann 2
Lucy 49
Polly 1

Simmons
Elizabeth Mansell 29
Polly 78
Susanna 84

Sledge
Betsy 90
Elizabeth 34,63
Milly 31
Patsy 46
Polly 85
Rebecca 42,78
Sarah 72
Susan 4

Smith
Betsy 60
Charity 88
Elizabeth 12,32,58

Smith (cont'd)
Frances 30,49
Lucy 21
Martha 29
Mary 22,54
Mildred 73
Nancy 49
Peggy 38
Permelia 67
Priscilla 9
Rebecca 88
Sally 43
Sarah 10,88
Selah 79
Susanna 18

Sarsby
Selah 29

Spain
Amy Gilliam 76
Elizabeth 77
Franky 84
Margaret 62
Mary 35
Nancy 84
Rebecca (3) 84

Stacy
Catharine 62,64
Caty 19
Hanna 62
Patsy 82
Rebecca 38

Stagg
Alice 44,58

Stephenson
Jincy 83

Stevens
Mary 62

Stewart
Ann 59
Lucretia 76
Nancy 39
Rebecca 54
Sarah 79
Scota 54

Stokes
Caty 87
Elizabeth 48
Lucy 60
Nancy 89

Stone
Ann H. 57

Stratson
Jinsey 76

Stuart
Elizabeth 28
Polly 53

Sturdivant		
Amy	37	
Anne	78	
Anney	37	
Betsy	46	
Dolly	64,90	
Edith	89	
Frances	57	
Lucy	25	
Polly	16,85	
Sykes		
Jane	2	
Judith	75	

T

Taylor	
Eliza	88
Elizabeth	13
Tharp	
Elizabeth	67
Mary Celia	26
Olive	26
Thomas	
Nancy	67
Sally	76
Thompson	
Mary Shaw	34
Threeweeks	
Frances	76
Thrift	
Susanna	11
Thweats	
Rebecca	25
Tilir	
Edney	30
Tomlinson	
Elizabeth	37,85
Frances	78
Lucy	20
Mary	88
Nancy E.	21
Patsey	77
Tucker	
Elizabeth	(2),87
Frances	49
Jane	86
Judith	13
Mary	87
Nancy	87
Tuder	
Livina	89
Lurana	71
Patsey	35
Rebecca	80
Sally	55

Tudor	
Amy	38
Turner	
Nancy	2
Tyus	
Cherry	29
Elizabeth Mary	39
Hanna	89
Nancy	36
Pamelia	39

U

Underhill	
Elizabeth	33
Mary	27,33
Mary Ann	69
Milley	17
Patsy	23
Rebecca	33
Sally	24
Underwood	
Rebecca	55
Silvia	25

V

Vaughan	
Ann	85
Dorothy	14,40
Elizabeth	(2),70
Martha	49
Velvin-Vilvan	
Nancy	12
Vincent	
Martha Hamlin	22
Vines	
Mary	4
Patsey	14
Vinson	
Betsy	47

W

Wade	
Peggy	21
Wakefield	
Nancy	27
Wall	
Sally D.	89
Wallace	
Rebecca	20,46
Waller	
Fanny	2
Sarah	1

Wallis	
Lucy	41
Peggy	45
Rebecca	46
Sarah	40
Sally D.	82
Wasdin	
Jincy	56
Wasdon	
Jesey	56
Watson	
Susan	76
Weathers	
Nancy	48
Polly	23
Weaver	
Lucy	27
Rebecca	69,72
Sally	27
Webb	
Ann	68
Elizabeth	86
Sarah	83
Welborne	
Betsy	50
Rebecca Bonner	71
Wells	
Elizabeth E.	83
White	
Avery	25
Avy	25
Clotilda	3
Diza	18
Elizabeth	40
Lucy	18
Mary	56
Nancy D.	83
Patsey	48
Rebecca	36
Sally	7
Willey	11
Whitehead	
Ann	71
Elizabeth	76
Whitehorn	
Elizabeth	57
Jincy	27
Patty	57
Polly	13
Whitfield	
Elizabeth	77
Martha	37
Mary	37
Nancy	46
Patty	37
Sally	55

Whittington
Nancy Smith 20
Patsy 85

Wiggins
Polly 74

Wilborne
Beckey 1
Jane 52
Nancy 85
Patsey 39
Polly 2,59
Rebecca 85
Temperance 80

Wilburne
Sarah 13

Wilkerson
Elizabeth 13
Mary 33
Polly 32
Rebecca 19,64
Susanna 17

Wilkinson
Nancy 12
Sarah 19

Wilcox-Willcox
Nancy 24
Ruth 45

Williams
Anne 49
Frances 36
Rebecca (2),49

Williamson
Ann 64
Elizabeth 17
Martha 49
Mima 1
Nancy 1
Rebecca (2),47
Sarah 29
Susanna 74
Temperance 62

Willis
Eleanor 81
Jacobina 44

Wilson
Jane 11

Winney
Susanna 6

Wingfield
Susanna 1

Winfield
Ann 61
Fanny 33
Lucrecy 64
Patty 33
Rebecca 51
Sally (2),24

Wood
Eliza S. 4

Woodard
Mary Wade 12
Nancy 48

Woodland
Mary 50
Phebey 5

Woodroof-Woodrooff
Catey 41
Elizabeth 58

Woodward
Keziah 13

Woolfolk
Elizabeth 9

Wooten-Wootten
Jane E. 36
Nancy 55
Sylvia 5

Wren-Wrenn
Clarissa 88
Elizabeth 15
Nancy 17
Polly 56
Sarah 66

Wright
Elizabeth 24

Wyatt
Agnes 86

Wyche
Ann 29
Elizabeth 15,68
Frances 68
Hannah 39
Leah 44
Martha 77
Mary Chapman 67
Rebecca 26

Wynne
Elizabeth 90
Frances 78,89
Lucrecy 58
Nancy 89
Peggy 46
Sally 77
Sarah 89
Susanna 89

Y

Yates
Elizabeth 15

Z

Zills
Ann 2,26
Mary 90

Zills (cont'd)
Nancy 83
Polly 1
Rebecca 39

www.ingramcontent.com/pod-product-compliance
Lightning Source LLC
Chambersburg PA
CBHW032044040426
42334CB00038B/658